TOM SHIELDS TAKES THE FIFTH

TOM SHIELDS

Tom Shields Takes The Fifth

Tom Shields
and Ken Smith

MAINSTREAM
PUBLISHING

EDINBURGH AND LONDON

First published in Great Britain in 2002 by
MAINSTREAM PUBLISHING COMPANY (EDINBURGH) LTD
7 Albany Street
Edinburgh EH1 3UG

ISBN 1 84018 688 7

A catalogue record for this book is available from the British Library

Typeset in Berkeley and Kartoon
Printed and bound in Great Britain by
The Bath Press, Bath

CONTENTS

FROM SCENES LIKE THESE

I have often been asked which is my favourite item from the years I spent cobbling together a Diary column for the *Glasgow Herald*. I used to reply: 'The next funny story somebody tells me.' Now that I have been released from the daily chore of collecting, reshaping, but mainly recycling, little nuggets for the benefit of *Herald* readers, I have had time to re-read some of the *bons mots*. I realise that my favourites tend to be those where the humour arises from the English language as it is used, abused, but generally improved by the Scots.

As a farewell thought, I offer my top ten wee stories, but not in any particular order. When being retold, these fragments are usually prefaced by the words: The scene is . . .

A Newton Mearns coffee shop where a lady is relating to her friends a rather nasty experience on a bus. 'This man sat down beside me and then he put his hand up my skirt. You know, the Jaeger one with the pleats . . .'

The dining-room of a cruise ship plying the Mediterranean hot-spots. One of the passengers is a Mr Bob Spiers, a Scotsman who is travelling alone. Mr Spiers is asked if he would mind sharing a table with a French gentleman who is also on his own. Mr Spiers speaks no French, the

Frenchman no English. At the first meal, the French chap says 'Bon appetit' to which the Scot replies 'Bob Spiers.' At the second and third meals, the Frenchman says 'Bon appetit' again, to which the Scot again replies 'Bob Spiers'. The ship's purser askes Mr Spiers how he is getting on with his table companion. 'He's a friendly enough chap,' replies Spiers, 'but he keeps forgetting we've met and introducing himself as "Bon Appetit".' The purser explains that this is French for 'enjoy your meal'.

Thus clued up, Mr Spiers greets his French companion at the next meal with the words 'Bon appetit'. The Frenchman smiles and replies: 'Bob Spiers.'

A Glasgow school where a letter has arrived addressed to a Mrs Youing. The staff quickly work out that it is intended for their Mrs Ewing. The letter is from a former pupil. Mrs Ewing wonders why he chose to write to her since she has never actually had the pleasure of teaching the young man. The letter makes it clear: 'I am writing to you because your name is the only one I can spell.'

Another Glasgow school where a teacher is taking a pupil to task for defacing his jotter cover with sectarian slogans. The teacher is, however, amused at the pupil's spelling of an oft-celebrated battle. The child had written: '1690. Remember the Boing.'

☆ ☆ ☆

A Glasgow office where a personnel person has been sent up from headquarters in England to interview staff for various posts, including that of junior clerical worker. One hopeful young lady enters the room, nervous but keen to make an impression as an outgoing and chatty sort of person. Pulling at her blouse, where perspiration is evident, she ventures the meteorological comment: 'Soafy clammy.' 'Come in, Miss Clammy. Take a seat,' says the personnel officer.

Kilwinning railway station where the stationmaster exhibits the inbred logic which has made the town renowned as Ayrshire's Burgh of Culture. A greyhound has escaped from the guard's van. The railway official chases it down the platform, shouting: 'Stoap that dug! It's a parcel!'

A Govan pub where a customer is informed that he has been rusticated, or barred as it is more commonly known. The man had been distressed to discover that his wife was having an affair and had tracked the philanderer to the pub, making a phone call. Our man proceeded to attack his rival in love with a machete. The victim suffered severe wounds to his arm. The attacker was barred, as the publican said in the indictment, for 'putting the phone out of order'.

The gents toilet of the Centre for Contemporary Arts, or the old Third Eye Centre as it is better known to senior citizens, where the following discussion is taking place:

    Man at first urinal: 'Spirituality is still an important element in society . . .'

    Man at second urinal: 'No, I doubt the relevance of spirituality in life today . . .'

    Voice from second cubicle on left: 'Surely, first of all you have to define spirituality . . .'

Greenock Sheriff Court, where an assault trial is in progress. The local newspaper, the *Greenock Telegraph*, as ever caught the flavour of the affray which had taken place during a social occasion in a Port Glasgow house. The report was headlined 'Sauce bottle attack victim needed 34 stitches'. A key part of the trial came when: 'Mrs Myra Rancier (36) told the court there had been an argument and Brownlie had punched Mrs

Findlay, knocking her over a chair. But she admitted she had not seen everything that had happened as she was blind in one eye, was drinking super lager, and had been reading *Bunty* comics at the time.'

A linguistics class in a university in Ontario, Canada. The professor tells the class: 'In English, a double negative forms a positive. In some languages, such as Russian, a double negative is still a negative. However, there is no language in which a double positive can form a negative.'

To which a Scots voice replies: 'Aye. Right.'

Tom Shields

WATERING HOLES

A hen night is noisily taking place in the Rat and Parrot bar in Glasgow, and eventually the girls decide it is time to move on. But one of them notices that they still have a bottle of house red which is nearly full. They decide to take it with them, but of course there is no cork to put in it as it had been opened by the bar staff. After a moment of thought, one of the ladies reaches into her handbag, unwraps a tampon and sticks it in the neck of the bottle. When it touches the alcohol it expands to fill the space and she happily pops the bottle into her cavernous bag sans spillage. Funny how they mention horse riding, swimming and skiing in the tampon advertisements, but never something as practical as this.

An Irish chap visiting Glasgow tells us about his encounter in a city-centre nightclub. Approaching a fair maiden with what he thought was a winning smile and the line: 'Would you like to dance with me?' he was met with the classy rejoinder: 'Take ma sister. Ah'm sweatin'.'

Towards the end of the Christmas party last year at a firm of Glasgow accountants, it became apparent that the glamorous new office start was

a) extremely drunk and b) game for a bit of fun with any of the bean-counters. Fearing for her safety and honour, the senior partner decided to drive her home himself, although a few miles out of his way, before going home to take his wife to her mother's. As men do, even when innocent, he failed to mention his earlier detour, but on the way to his mother-in-law's he happened to spot, in the light of the passing street lamps, a shoe in the passenger well of his car. Diverting his wife's attention, he grabbed the shoe and furtively deposited it out the car window when he stopped at some traffic lights. Pleased with himself that he had saved the day, he was astonished on arrival to hear his wife inquire: 'Do you see my other shoe?'

☆ ☆ ☆

We hear of a pub in Milngavie where the regulars' enjoyment of sporting broadcasts is occasionally spoiled by the fact that the sound on the telly is knackered (a technical term there). Normal service is usually restored by the barmaid thumping vigorously on the side of the TV set. The barmaid came into the bar to find an Old Firm game on but no sound emanating from the TV. She proceeded to use her TV repair skills only to be asked by the customers to desist from her bashing as it was kind of spoiling the effect of the minute's silence for Jim Baxter.

☆ ☆ ☆

Fred Emden, the bar manager at the Tron Theatre in Glasgow, perhaps takes those questionnaires in magazines a little bit too seriously. He was asked a series of standard questions for the arts publication *Live & Direct*, and under 'What three things could you not live without?' eschewed the usual luvviedom answers such as Shakespeare or my music collection, by answering with the more literal: 'Heart, liver, and kidneys.'

☆ ☆ ☆

Colin Barr is well known in Glasgow for his trendy pubs and

clubs. A fellow businessman who was invited to his house once, like many others, admired the large stylish mirror on display with the letters CB through it. Inquiring how much it would cost to have such an individual mirror made, Colin eventually admitted that he had bought it from a City Bakeries that was closing down.

A couple of chaps aff a boat are having a wee soirée in Invergordon. After several drinks they discover that there is an Indian restaurant in Alness and, appetites sharpened, they jump in a taxi. On arrival, one gives the driver a tenner and tells him to keep the change. His mate observes: 'That was a bit expensive for a ten-minute journey.' 'Well, it said £9.50 on the meter,' says the first. It is then his friend gives him some useful information – Invergordon taxis do not in fact have meters, but they do have clocks.

A good citizen of Coatbridge claims he was in his local when the punter next to him attracted the barmaid's attention and protested loudly that his pint was cloudy. The provider of ales took a careful look at his pint then came to the conclusion: 'Naw, ye're wrang. It's jist that the glass is durty.' This seemed to satisfy the thirsty customer who informed her: 'That's awright then, hen. Jist is long is the beer isnae cloudy.'

Some overheard snatches of conversation just have to be passed on. Such as the discussion on films in a south-side-of-Glasgow pub, where one of the group explains: 'Aye, you know, *In The Heat of the Night* – it's the one where Sidney Poitier plays a black man.'

The scene is a Glasgow pub, where the peace of a Sunday evening is shattered by the arrival of a lady the worse for wear and the worse for drink. A latter-day Edna the inebriate, she begins to harangue the barman. Among the customers desultorily watching the proceedings is a 6 ft 6 in. chap in a frock who is pursuing a transvestite lifestyle, but still likes a pint in his/her local. Another regular customer leans over to the chap in the frock and says: 'And you want to be a woman?'

☆ ☆ ☆

Even workmen can be sensitive. A new bar, Cuba Norte, was opening in the Merchant City and the shopfitter sent in had to pull up a nasty acrylic carpet. Underneath he found a beautiful marble floor. Or as he was heard to put it: 'That's disgusting. It's like putting a Hallowe'en mask on Claudia Schiffer.'

☆ ☆ ☆

An office Christmas do was taking place in a big Glasgow hotel, and the service was less than perfect – there was a double booking, tables squeezed in, and food running out. At last, the weary waitress, from the school-dinner style of catering, said hands up those who wanted coffee. Everyone's hand went up, except one girl who said she didn't want anything. Eventually, after coaxing from the waitress, she finally said she would have a cup of tea, but was clearly embarrassed by all the attention. So to put her at her ease, the cheery waitress told her: 'It's OK, hen, don't worry. Ah'm the same. Any time Ah go anywhere, Ah'm a pain in the arse as well.'

A visitor to Ayr was having trouble finding the town's popular Brig O'Doon Hotel. He stopped the ubiquitous wifie and asked where he would find the Alloway turn-off. 'He's at hame, son, I married him 22 years ago,' came the swift response.

Dining out, Glasgow-style. A chap in a city-centre Italian restaurant orders a steak. Minutes later the waiter replaces the knife in front of him with a fearsome-looking steak knife. The diner, perhaps in a foolish attempt to impress his dining companion by engaging in harmless banter with the waiter, says in a loud voice: 'So, are the steaks tough in here?' But the Italian server merely replies: 'Not as tough as the waiters,' before gliding away.

On the theme of misunderstandings in a restaurant, a Glasgow chap is still blushing recalling the time he was trying to impress a young lady by taking her to a Greek restaurant. The waiter, authentically Greek, is taking their order. The Glasgow chap, taking control, orders a carafe of house wine. 'Litre?' asks the waiter. 'No,' says the man, a bit puzzled, 'can you just bring it now?'

The scene is a restaurant in Inveraray, where a young waiter – enthusiastic, hardworking, but, alas, untrained – is serving a couple. The man orders a fillet steak. 'I'll just pop into the kitchen and make sure there is a fillet steak left,' says the waiter. He returns to confirm that fillet steak is available. 'Well done,' says the customer. 'Thanks, but it's all right. It's my job,' replies the waiter, modestly declining praise. 'I'd like my steak well done,' says the customer, in a firm tone.

St Patrick's Day celebrations in Glasgow, and we overhear an Irishman in a pub who has obviously decided to be a professional jokester for the day. He asks for a whisky and water, and after taking a sip asks the barman: 'Which did you put in

first?' 'The whisky,' the puzzled barman replies. Which gives our chap the chance to say in a loud voice to an appreciative audience: 'Ah, well, no doubt I'll get to it eventually.'

A conversation last week between two old worthies in the Fountain Bar in Edinburgh, when the subject of sleeping patterns – a common obsession among senior citizens, we hear – becomes the topic of the day. One chap says he sleeps with the window open, but his pal tells him: 'So dae Ah, but Ah get woken up wae the dawn chorus.' To which the other chap replies: 'Ah don't know about any chorus – it's thae bluidy birds that wake me up.'

A chap in a West End bar is observed draining his pint then telling his mate: 'The wife thinks I'm too nosey.' So his pal asks: 'When did she say that?' 'Oh no,' the chap explains. 'She never actually told me. I read it in her diary.'

A black-tie dinner was held at the Hilton in Glasgow, raising money for the Maggie Centre opening in the city. The harassed waiters and waitresses were trying to serve more than 500 hungry diners at once. At one table, a chap looked suspiciously at his lamb and told the waitress that he had ordered it to be pink. The waitress, who had gone on to serve broadcaster Kirsty Wark, returned to the gentleman and told him: 'See if you squeeze your beetroot over it, it'll turn pink,' and returned to her busy job.

IN THE BACK OF MY CABIN

A taxi driver – and who are we to doubt them? – tells of picking up an elderly lady at a Glasgow city-centre pub on a freezing winter's night. The old dear asked to be taken to the Orange Hall in Maryhill. Making conversation, the driver says: 'Bitter,' to which she replies: 'No me. I'm just going to play bingo.'

A group of Glasgow taxi drivers had gone to St Andrews to play the Old Course. Thinking that gave them access to the venerable and crusty Royal & Ancient Golf Club beside the course, one of them strolled in, and conversationally said 'Lovely morning' to a stern-looking chap in an armchair who completely ignored him. Moments later a waiter arrived, and the chap in the chair loudly clicked his fingers to attract his attention. The waiter went over and was told: 'Chap over there wants to discuss the weather. Oblige him.'

A Glasgow taxi driver is still shaking his head after being asked by a businessman visiting the city to take him to an Italian-sounding boozer called Albaroni, which the chap had been carousing in the night before and wanted to return to. The driver had never heard of it, neither had

other drivers, nor his controller, but in desperation the chap told him to drive around the city centre until he excitedly spotted it. The premises were in fact All Bar One.

☆ ☆ ☆

Regulars at the redoubtable Lochy Bar in Caol, near Fort William, recall the 'Taxi for Macauley' incident, and no, unlike every programme BBC Scotland is making these days, it did not involve comedian Fred Macauley. Instead, it was the chap who, after a few halfs, telephoned the local taxi firm. But when the driver came in the door and shouted 'Taxi for Macauley', there was no one of that name. Eventually the chap in the corner, a crofter, got to

his feet, handed the driver a fiver, and his collie dog on a lead, and told him to take 'ma collie' back to his croft at Banavie while he stayed on for a few more drinks. 'Taxi for ma collie' is now a regular saying in the Lochy.

☆ ☆ ☆

Further examples of the accidental perspicacity of Glasgow taxi drivers. We are told of a woman getting in a cab outside the supermarket, her shopping bulging with the ingredients to cook a Mexican meal. 'Chilly tonight,' the driver said conversationally, to which the passenger replied: 'How did you know?'

☆ ☆ ☆

IN THE BACK OF MY CABIN

A former Glasgow University student living in Summerston, to give north Maryhill its Sunday name, has put on his dinner jacket and bow tie to attend a dinner at the uni. The taxi driver he hailed, to make conversation, asked if he was indeed going to a dinner. The chap answered in the affirmative, but then foolishly added: 'How did you know?' The taxi driver, with barely a pause, told him: 'We don't pick up that many penguins this side of the Antarctic.'

We are told by a Glasgow taxi driver – so it must be true – that he was flagged down outside the Royal Infirmary by a young man in a smart suit drinking a bottle of Budweiser and carrying a rifle in his other hand. The bemused driver put down his window and told him: 'You can't bring that in here.' The young man-at-arms told him: 'I know. I'll finish it before I get in,' and promptly drained the bottle of Bud.

A taxi driver tells us he arrived at a Glasgow West End address where a cocktail party was in full swing. Walking to the close door (this is an old-fashioned taxi driver who actually gets out of his cab rather than just blasting his horn in the small hours, but we digress) he noticed the entry buzzer was not working. There was a note stuck to it stating: 'If ingress cannot be achieved, please use the ski pole and tap the nearest window.' Sure enough there was a ski pole, which indeed had the desired effect. It was later he reflected that only in the West End would they use the word 'ingress', and have a ski pole lying about.

JOB13Y LOT

We hear of four Falkirk businessmen in the town's Scotia Bar discussing an up-and-coming golf outing to Washington, Tyne and Wear. There is much argument about the distance involved, which allows one of them smugly to suggest he could check it on his spanking new Mercedes which has satellite navigation. He returns to tell them the distance is 90 miles. But one of them is not convinced. He declares that Edinburgh to Newcastle alone is more than that, so from Falkirk it has to be further. So the only way to settle it was for all four to troop out to the Merc where the proud owner says: 'See, 89.9 miles.' It is then an eagle-eyed pal points out he is reading the frequency of BBC Radio 2, and not the satellite navigation readout. The owner's face, it is said, was redder than a Ferrari.

Two shell-suited Glasgow chaps were whiling away their bank holiday by sitting on a wall watching the world go by when a car drove up with a German tourist looking for directions. 'Entschuldigung, koennen sie Deutsch sprechen?' he asks, but the two lads just stared at him. He then tried: 'Excusez-moi, parlez vous Francais?' but the stares continued. Then 'Parla Italiano?' followed by 'Hablan ustedes Espanol?' got him nowhere before he finally drove off in exasperation. So one of the lads said: 'Do you no' think we should a stuck in at school and learned a foreign language?' 'Why?' said his mate. 'That guy knew four languages – and it didnae do him any good.'

Diary reader Germaine Stafford works for the US Navy and is based in Naples, where the base newspaper contained the following advertisement: 'For sale, double sofa bed, $40.00. Legs slightly wobbly, mattress hard and lumpy. Suitable for in-laws.'

☆ ☆ ☆

Someone not clear on the concept. An elderly gentleman attempting to enter Tesco in Forfar at 10.30 a.m. on Tuesday, shortly after a prayer session in a nearby church for the Queen Mother, was turned away. When he inquired why, he was told by staff that it was 'for the Queen Mother'. Temporarily baffled, the chap replied: 'I didn't know she shopped here.'

☆ ☆ ☆

A woman is explaining to her friend that she heard on the radio that there is a competition in Glasgow where people take part in Irish dancing which lasts only 30 seconds. There is a lengthy discussion about what kind of routine you could do in half-a-minute, and did that mean they went incredibly fast? Further enlightenment comes the following day when a newspaper reports that Glasgow is playing host to the 32nd International Irish Dancing Championships.

☆ ☆ ☆

We hear of the folk on the Orkney island of Rousay who held a dance to raise funds to remove the unsightly abandoned cars, fridges and so on which litter the sides of the roads. Unfortunately, although the dance was a big success, it had to be halted due to a bit of a rammy among some of the young men attending. The name of the event? Yes, The Scrap Dance.

Something to ponder? The Japanese eat very little fat and suffer fewer heart attacks than the British or Americans. On the other hand, the French eat a lot of fat and also suffer fewer heart attacks than the British or

Americans. The Italians drink excessive amounts of red wine, and also suffer fewer heart attacks than the British or Americans. Conclusion? Eat and drink what you like. It's speaking English that kills you.

Loath as we are to contribute to the suggestion that disc jockeys are not the sharpest knives in the drawer, we must pass on the story of Radio Clyde's George Bowie at a promotions night at the Phoenix Honda showroom in Linwood. George is passed a note so that he can ask over the microphone if the owner of a certain car, and he gives out the registration, could return to the vehicle and switch off his lights, which have been left on. At the end of the night George troops out to his own car and discovers a flat battery. Yes, he had been reading out his own registration.

There is nothing worse for serious punters than hearing of folk choosing horses for the daftest of reasons. An about-to-be-married young woman from Edinburgh taken to Cheltenham for the Gold Cup by her fiancé explained that she had picked the winner, Best Mate, because of the trainer, the excitable Henrietta Knight, who cannot even face watching races her horses are competing in. When asked to explain, she said that Henrietta is known by the shortened name of Hen. When that still didn't make sense she added: 'Hen. Hen night.'

Bentwood
easy-chairs were
£60.00
**half price
£25.00**

Ingenious, if slightly potty, number plate spotted in Glasgow on a van belonging to Grant's, an emergency plumber: JOB13Y. They have merged the two numbers to create the letter B.

A slightly infelicitous choice of phrase in *BA News*, the magazine of British Airways. Heroic former New York mayor Rudy Giuliani flew to London on Concorde to collect his honorary knighthood for efforts on and after the events of 11 September. The magazine reported: 'He was presented with a souvenir British Airways cap and bomber jacket on arrival at Heathrow.'

A Greenock lady swears blind that her husband wanted a favourite shirt washed for a special occasion, so she decided to put her foot down and told him to wash it himself. From the kitchen came a cry of: 'What setting do I use?' When she shouted back: 'What does it say on the shirt?', there was a pause before he retorted with 'Ben Sherman'.

A chap from Glasgow tells us he was among shinty folk on Skye for the annual Camanachd Dinner Dance at the Gathering Hall in Portree. He was sitting next to an aged local, known for his piscatorial prowess as well as his shinty-playing in his younger days, who picked up the menu, read that the main course was poached salmon, and remarked to no one in particular: 'Is there any other type?'

How public attitudes change. A smoker tells us he joined the other would-be passengers huddling from the rain under the bus shelter outside the RSAMD in Renfrew Street, Glasgow, and lit up a cigarette. As the smoke drifted across the others, one chap told him: 'This is a no-smoking bus shelter.' He actually stubbed out his fag before he realised there is no such thing.

They breed them tough in Lanarkshire's Bellshill. A Diary correspondent was the sole customer in a chip shop in the town when a drunk swayed in and asked him for a light, but our chap explained he did not smoke. Becoming a bit testy, the drunk then asked the chip-shop owner for a light, but, again, his request was answered in the negative. So the inebriated chap pointed at the fat-fryer and said: 'Well how do you light that?' 'Automatic pilot,' replied the owner. At that the drunk turned on his heel in disgust and, while lurching out the door, bawled back: 'I've a good mind to torch your shop,' to which the owner, without a pause, calmly replied: 'You can't. You've not got a light.'

The Hemp Paper Company in Turriff, Aberdeenshire, does indeed make wallpapers from hemp, or *cannabis sativa* to give it its Sunday name, and this is forecast to become the very latest in style. The company says there are huge environmental savings in using hemp, and that it produces wallpaper of character, strength and versatility. But they haven't forgotten their native Aberdeenshire canniness. The company states on its labels: 'Please do not attempt to smoke the wallpaper. It contains no active ingredient and will only give you a headache.' Ah, but can you cover schoolbooks with it, Glasgow schoolchildren anxiously wait to hear.

A recent staging of the poignant play *Sons of Ulster Marching to the Somme* at Glasgow's Citizens' Theatre reminded reader Norma McGovern of when it was on at the Rep in Dundee. At the bar afterwards, one of the actors came round gasping for a pint. The barmaid, in that cheerful way they do, said he'd missed last orders. Hoping that appearing in the play might make a difference, he told her: 'But I'm one of the Sons of Ulster.' Without batting an eyelid she replied: 'Eh don't care if you are the Son of God, you ain't getting served.'

ROMANCE

A Valentine's Day survey revealed that most married men fantasise that their wives aren't fantasising.

Women in Glasgow's West End are becoming, quite rightly, more suspicious. We overheard a chap in a pub asking a young woman out for a meal. After grudgingly agreeing, she then fixed him with a stare and told him: 'Just to clarify – meal doesn't qualify if a) the word "happy" is in front of it, b) cutlery is not obligatory and c) the phrases "carry out" or "take-away" appear on the same line.'

Craig Dean of Hamilton confesses that he awoke one St Valentine's Day with a stunning hangover when his then girlfriend came into the room with tea and toast on a tray. On picking up the toast, his bleary eye noticed it wasn't its normal rectangular shape, so he blurted out: 'Have you had a bite oot ma toast, ya greedy pig?' Imagine his horror when she frostily replied: 'No. I shaped it into a Valentine's heart for you.' Well, as we said earlier, the phrase 'then girlfriend' is a clue to what happened after that.

Glasgow University's *Guardian* newspaper carries suggestions as to what single students might be doing on Valentine's Day. They range from the philosophical 'propping up the bar in The Garage nightclub, wondering how many discounted drinks are required to attain the levels of "fun" promised by advertising flyers', to the simply sad: 'Burning all letters and photos from ex-girlfriends in a tearful, whisky-fuelled rage then desperately trying to stamp out the flames, having changed his mind halfway through.'

☆ ☆ ☆

Theo de Voogd of Dumbarton tells us of trying to kill two birds with one stone by making up to his wife after days of non-communication with a present on St Valentine's Day. He went to the florists for a single rose, the corner shop for some chocolates, and the local ladieswear shop for a pair of fashionable stockings. He left them on the table on the morning of the 14th and, on arriving home in the evening, was delighted to see the rose on the mantelpiece and the box of chocolates open. He then gazed at his wife's legs and told her: 'Oh dear, sorry about the colour of the stockings, they looked a nicer shade on the packet.' The evening then went horribly wrong as his wife coldly explained that she wasn't wearing any stockings.

☆ ☆ ☆

If there can be such a thing as a one-way dialogue then it is surely that reported to us between an Ayrshire couple in the twilight of their years. Their years of marriage had been characterised by conversations in which she would attempt to obtain from him information or guidance, usually in vain. 'What do you want in your piece?' 'Och, anything at all.' 'What would you like for your tea?' 'Whatever

you're having.' Then, one evening, came the question about how he would like to go, when his time came. 'Would you like to be buried or cremated?' she asked. 'I'm no really bothered,' he replied. 'I'll need to know,' the wife insisted. Resorting to a tactic which we suspect he had used before, the man said: 'Just surprise me.'

DEAR DEPARTED

The Diary had to say farewell to some great Scots who will hopefully stay warm in our memories for some time to come.

The Donald Dewar stories that have filtered into the Diary reflect the affection people felt for the man. His lack of pomposity often features, like the time he received a phone call from the BBC. They were making a drama in which a policeman entered a room and said the line: 'Switch off that TV. What's that boring nonsense you were watching anyway?' The TV clip in question was Donald talking about devolution and the programme-makers were seeking his permission to use it. Donald, ever the gentleman, agreed.

One of his official engagements took him to a Kwik-Fit centre which was being used as a collection centre for a Kosovo charity. Shunning the official limo, Donald drove there in his less-than-flash N-registration Peugeot. As Donald performed his stately duties he saw his old Peugeot being driven into a bay. A very quick Kwik-Fit fitter had assumed it was an old banger in for a free brakes check.

Donald's egregious facial features made him a target for lookalike suggestions: the teacher in the 'Oor Wullie' cartoon strip, and a character called The Cleaner in *Toy Story 2*. But Mr Dewar was not unattractive to the ladies – when female staff in the House of Commons were asked to

name the most fanciable men at Westminster, Donald was towards the top of the poll. A secretary to a Conservative MP described him as 'very much a Heathcliff figure'. This accolade would probably have meant nothing to Donald, the man who, when told that a meeting was to take place on St Valentine's Day, asked: 'When's that?'

His fondness for Jaffa Cakes and other sweetmeats was regularly chronicled in this column. Once, as First Minister, he was spotted at a lunch pocketing two lumps of tablet from the table at which he had stopped to engage colleagues in conversation. 'Is Donald getting greedy?' someone asked. 'No,' said another colleague, 'it's just that he has to take a bit back for Jim Wallace, his deputy.'

☆ ☆ ☆

The affectionate memories of Donald Dewar continued on the anniversary of his death. Tony Hughes in Prestonpans recalled that after Donald's death a local radio reporter was interviewing people on what Donald's legacy would be. But perhaps not explaining the concept clearly, he asked a Labour Club official: 'What did Donald Dewar leave behind?' He was then told: 'Donald came through to the club for a Burns Supper once, and after his plate of broth he asked if there was any more. So he had more broth, then came the haggis, tatties and neeps. After eating that he asked if there was any left, so he had another helping. Then he ate three desserts. So you could say he left behind a lot of plates.' We don't think the interview was used, but then again, we don't believe Donald would have minded.

☆ ☆ ☆

Our favourite story about the late John McGrath is the oft-told one about him stopping at a filling station near Perth after being up north with the 7:84 theatre company. At the time he was driving a Volvo estate which was needed to help transport props and costumes around. The young chap filling the tank saw the 7:84 sticker, asked what it was, and John explained that it was making the point that 84 per cent of Great Britain's wealth is owned by only 7 per cent of the population. The young chap, having a quick glance at the Volvo, told him: 'There's no need to show off about it.'

Glasgow Lord Provost Alex Mosson was delighted to help plant a cherry tree and unveil a plaque to entertainer Jimmy Logan in the city's Botanic Gardens. Alex attended a charity dinner Jimmy was at just a few weeks before he died, and Jimmy had recalled on the night how he was taken to Belfast when he was a little boy and was enjoying the jaunt in the car, sitting with a large overweight driver and two nuns. The big chap passed wind loudly, and felt he had to apologise to the nuns. Jimmy could still recall that one of the nuns replied: 'Don't worry. We thought it was the horses.' Mary Lee, widow of fellow entertainer Jack Milroy, who also attended the unveiling, says there has been talk of putting up a plaque in Jack's memory too. She suggested putting it outside the local bookies as he spent so much time there. And she wasn't joking. She was amused to see that the

bookies put on a minibus to take regulars to Jack's funeral.

Panto star Johnny Beattie, who describes Glasgow's Botanic Gardens as his back garden, also popped over for the unveiling of the plaque. He said it is often forgotten that Jimmy made and lost a number of fortunes. At one time he even had his own plane, which he was proud to pilot. He took his mother up in the air and was banking the plane slightly, and telling her: 'Look over to the right, there's the Ailsa Craig, and over to the left, that's Girvan.' His mother, hanging on to the front of her seat, told him: 'Oh son, just keep your eye on the road.'

☆ ☆ ☆

The last time we met Jack Milroy he was busy disrupting his partner-in-mirth Rikki Fulton's book launch. Mr Milroy told the Diary that he, too, was engaged upon writing his autobiography. 'I'm at page 14,' he said. 'And I've covered the bit where I move from Coplaw Street in Govanhill to Shawlands. You may ask how can it take 14 pages to move from Govanhill to Shawlands when it's only four stops on the bus,' Mr Milroy said. He answered the question himself, of course: 'The traffic's terrible on the Victoria Road.'

☆ ☆ ☆

Jack Milroy's cremation was not so much a funeral as a celebration of the life of one of the kings of

Scottish comedy. Johnny Beattie told of driving past the crematorium with Jack a few weeks before his death. 'When I go that's where I want to go from. It's got a rare view doon the watter,' Jack declared. And Billy Differ, now in the theatre business in London, told of Jack going to the Palace to get his MBE wearing a kilt and his old tap shoes: 'We did not see the wee man coming but we could hear him a mile away.' Rikki Fulton, for decades Josie to Milroy's Francie, spoke of a true gentleman and a great friend but said that he had to take over their financial affairs when Jack described some cash stolen from their dressing-room in Ireland as 'only money, china . . .'

☆ ☆ ☆

The great and the good have given their tributes to Tom Winning, but we wish to record The Diary's appreciation of the cardinal's willingness to go along with our own curious way of looking at life. Although inundated with inquiries when he became cardinal, Tom took time to answer The Diary's questions. When we asked what the new job meant, he said: 'I'm told the word cardinal derives from the Latin for "hinge". Someone told me a hinge works best when it is well-oiled but I don't think that applies to cardinals.' We asked what were the cardinal sins and the cardinal virtues, and he told us: 'I've forgotten. I would need to check in the

Catechism. I'm looking forward to dropping in on Cardinal Sin when I'm out in Australia for the beatification of Mary McKillop.' When we asked about the chances of further promotion he joked: 'It is said in Rome that the Cardinal of Milan is destined to change from martini rosso to martini bianco.' And on Craigneuk, his home village, he cheerily told us: 'I still go back. I noticed that an Orange hall has been built on the site of the house where I was born and brought up.' Naturally we asked: 'Does that mean there will be a problem with where to put the plaque?' Typical of the man, he replied: 'Who needs a plaque?' Fame was never his interest. When we cheekily asked if he was the most famous person to come out of Craigneuk, Tom replied: 'Only if you don't count Lisbon Lion Tommy Gemmell and boxers Chic Calderwood and Tommy Milligan.' Many could learn from his modesty. Thanks Tom.

KIDS

Ah, the little ones. A nursery school in Lanarkshire always celebrates birthdays, and this day it was the turn of a member of staff who had reached the ripe old age of 22. After school she was shopping in the local Co-op when a mother of one of her charges came up and asked if it was true it was her birthday. When the teacher said yes, the mother asked: 'What age are you?' '22,' she replied. 'Ah,' said the mother, 'when Cameron came home he said you were five to four.'

A Glasgow father is watching over his young daughter's shoulder as she sets up an e-mail account on the family computer. She reaches the point where she has to put in a password and the message on the screen says that it has to have at least four characters. So, after thinking about it, she types in 'snowwhitebartsimpsonshrekwoodie'.

Baffling, indeed, are the conversations that you hear on public transport. Two expensively dressed teenage girls are travelling on the Glasgow to Bearsden train and the exchange goes: 'You mean you buy your own clothes?' 'Yes.' 'All your clothes?' 'Yes.' 'Really . . . you mean you actually buy all your own clothes?' 'Yes – but I steal all my make-up.'

A further slice of Glasgow life is overheard on the No. 75 bus from Castlemilk into the town, where a little girl is whispering to her mum, who eventually declares: 'Wha? You don't want mammy to have a baby, stupid.' The toddler insists that she does, so Mum tells her: 'I told you, you need a man to have a baby and Mammy hasn't got a man.' So the little girl changes tack and asks if they can get a daddy, to which her thoughtful mother replies: 'Wha? You want a baby and a daddy? Now you're just being greedy.'

A reader tells us of a busy Santa's grotto where a little chap is perched on Santa's knee rhyming off the long list of gadgets he wants. The old, bearded fellow unexpectedly breaks wind, and in an attempt to save Santa's blushes, the boy's mother says: 'Gosh, Santa, you'll have to stop feeding your reindeer baked beans for their tea.' Her valiant attempt is spoiled by her son, who shouts excitedly: 'Santa farted! And it smells like rotten eggs.' Suddenly someone's face was as red as his outfit.

A couple from Airdrie on holiday with their eight-year-old son in the Med notice that women at the pool are sunbathing topless. As Airdrie is not noted for its topless facilities, this is obviously something young Tommy has not seen before. His mum, fearing the lad might make some loud and embarrassing remark, dispatches her husband to have a word with him. 'Son,' says the father in a man-to-man manner, 'you know, there are one or two ladies out there who are topless.' 'Naw, Daddy,' replies young Tommy, 'there's 12 of them!'

☆ ☆ ☆

It's a terrible day when you can't believe teachers, but we have our doubts about the one who tells us about the eight-year-old in her class who was constantly scratching his groin area. When she asked what the problem was, the little lad said he had a pimple down there and it was extremely itchy. Seeing he had a problem with it, she took him to the school office to telephone his mother to see what she wanted him to do. A few minutes later the boy returned to the classroom with his fly open and his willie hanging out. The teacher was taken aback and asked what his mother had said. He told her: 'She said that I have to stick it out till lunchtime and if the itch is still there then I can go home.'

Sometimes they just ask for it. A primary-school teacher in the Borders tells us how she was teaching her class about the Vikings. 'Now,' she said, hoping to make the lesson a little more vivid, 'what do you think was the first thing a Viking would have said when he arrived in Britain?' A young chap at the back of the class stuck his hand up and proceeded to make bizarre hacking and spluttering noises. It took a moment for her to realise that, true to the question, he was offering his best approximation of Danish.

At a Boys' Brigade camp, the captain is talking to the lads about how they would survive if they were lost and alone in the desert. He asks what would be the three most important things to have with you. After much thought, one lad sticks up his hand and says: 'Water, a compass and a deck of cards.' Puzzled as to why he would take cards with him, the skipper asks for an explanation. 'Well, sir,' said the boy, 'as soon as you start playing solitaire, someone is bound to come up behind you and say, "Put that red nine on top of that black ten."'

☆ ☆ ☆

An educational psychologist swears it is true that, at a nursery in Lanarkshire, he asked a little boy to draw a man. The puzzled psychologist noted that only the body and crude representations of arms and legs were produced, so he said to the boy: 'Why don't you put the head on it?' The young chap looked thoughtful, shrugged his shoulders, then head-butted the paper on the table.

☆ ☆ ☆

Scene in the organisers' tent at the Edinburgh Book Festival. A child, one of many little darlings who are such a delight in the festival's tented village, entered and said: 'I can't find my mummy.' 'We have a lost child here,' cried an organiser. 'No,' replied the child sternly, 'what we have is a lost mummy.'

☆ ☆ ☆

A mother who moved to Newton Mearns recently found that her son still wanted his hot-water bottle, shaped like a cat, in bed at night to comfort him in the strange surroundings. That was why when the local minister called round to welcome her to the area, a voice from upstairs in the bedroom shouted down: 'I want hot pussy.' For some reason the conversation with the minister seemed a bit strained after that.

We hear of an elegant primary seven teacher in an East Renfrewshire school who was returning the class's language jotters after marking. Unhappy with the work one child had produced she leant over his desk and said quietly: 'Half-hearted,' then placed the jotter in front of him. He looked at her wide-eyed, turned to his pal and said incredulously: 'She said she's farted.'

Cute-kids' stories? We can never get enough of them. Robin Veitch, president of Clydebank Rugby Club, was telephoning the match secretary of another club, only to have the call answered by a very young voice. 'Is your mummy or daddy there?' inquired Robin. 'No,' said the youngster who had been well taught, as he or she added: 'Can I take a message?' After Robin confirmed with the little one that he or she had a pencil and paper, he said: 'Robin called,' and added to be helpful: 'R-O-B-I-N.' After a pause the little voice asked him: 'How do you make an R?'

PUBLIC
TOILETS

P

WITHIN THE
LINES ONLY

An Edinburgh couple were happily driving through the countryside past an idyllic view of a field of cows when their little daughter piped up from the child seat in the back: 'Daddy, why are these cows not on fire?' They agreed that perhaps they should cut down on the number of foot-and-mouth news items she was watching on the telly.

☆ ☆ ☆

A Glasgow West End couple, keen to expand the knowledge of their young daughter, took her for her first Chinese meal. They wanted a hole to swallow them up, however, when the young thing exclaimed loudly that the restaurant served snakes and rats. Telling her to be quiet, they quickly explained, as liberal parents do, that there were many myths about Chinese restaurants but it was bad of her to repeat what they thought was playground tittle-tattle. It was only after their daughter insisted it was in the menu that they discovered she was reading about the Chinese zodiac.

☆ ☆ ☆

A sign of the times, as they say. A couple who called in at the Mishnish Hotel in Tobermory at the Easter weekend got chatting to the woman at the next table and her little girl. Eventually one of them asked the wee one how old she was, to which she replied: 'Six. But if I am on the ferry or train I am only four.'

☆ ☆ ☆

A Bearsden couple were playing I-Spy with their five-year-old daughter when she announced: 'Something beginning with W.' They tried 'wall', 'window', and so on until they were stumped.

So their daughter gave them a clue. 'It's something that all daddies have.' As the girl's dad told us: 'Great minds think alike, and my wife and I looked aghast at each other as we dreaded what kind of vocabulary Hilary was acquiring in her first year at school or, indeed, what she might be spying.' A double sigh of relief was expressed when Hilary explained that the answer was, of course, 'Wallet.'

Sights seen in Glasgow's West End, rarely seen elsewhere. A portrait photographer has a large model cow that she uses to pose children upon. She decides to take it outside for a spring-clean, and is seen by a workman opposite enthusiastically thrashing the dust out of it with a carpet-beater. 'Haw missis,' he cries, 'It's no the coo's fault it's got foot-and-mouth disease.'

We assume it was a different worker who arrived at a houseproud West-Ender's house to repair a window just after she had washed the kitchen floor. 'Hang on a minute,' she said, 'while I put some newspapers down.' 'It's all right dear,' he told her, 'I'm house-trained.'

We have all seen warnings attached to toys and appliances which state the blindingly obvious. It would be nice if the warnings were far more accurate at Christmas time, such as: 'Action Man: Warning – "action figure" is a euphemism. It is still a dolly.' 'Pokemon: This toy will result in your first addiction. Cigarettes, alcohol, marijuana, cocaine and heroin will inevitably follow.' 'Yo-yo: Regardless of skill level, use of this product can never make you look good.' 'Mini-scooter: Will instantly render you indistinguishable from every other child in the country.' 'Playstation 2: Not intended as a parental substitute. May stunt social growth. Increased popularity among your peers is only temporary.'

No, not all the Ayrshire school stories have been exhausted. Another teacher tells us of a double period at a secondary school which straddled the lunch break. In the afternoon period there was a chap in class who wasn't there in the morning. Asked where he had been, he replies: 'Sorry sur, a wis et the fish school.' The teacher racks his brain, wondering if he had missed a new and unusual vocational initiative. 'The fish school, eh? What kind of things do you do there?' he inquires, his brain now whirling with thoughts of fly-tying or gutting. 'Naw, sur,' replies the exasperated pupil. 'The procurator fishschool – ah got lifted at the weekend.'

A teacher takes us to task for suggesting in our tales from Ayrshire schools that the progeny of that fair region can sometimes be a tad uncouth and unworldly. He points out that some of the suburbs of Ayr are extremely middle class. He offers as proof the fact that in one primary school pupils were surveyed on various matters, and under 'most disliked household chore', the top answer was 'washing the patio furniture'.

A Glasgow chap is left alone at home by his wife and settles down in front of the telly. The doorbell goes. It is children out guising for Hallowe'en. He's a bit stressed as it is usually his wife who deals with this kind of thing, but he invites them in, they do their party piece, and he goes into the kitchen to find something to reward them with. The kitchen is, of course, a foreign country. All he can find are six kiwi fruits, which he dispenses to the little ones, along with the change from his pocket. As he closes the door, the little girl dressed as an angel comes out with the less than angelic: 'What the hell is this?' He returns to armchair, pondering on the fact that his neighbours will now be thinking: 'Who are these stuck-up so-and-sos at number 12 who give out kiwi fruit at Hallowe'en?' Being male, he comforts himself with the fact that it's all his wife's fault for going out.

The government's latest campaign against truancy prompted Duncan Johnston to tell us about his brother-in-law working at a school where the phone rang and a suspiciously young voice said that a certain pupil would not be at school that day as he was sick. The secretary thanked the caller and asked who was phoning. The caller replied: 'My dad.'

A school photographer was arranging dates with a nursery head teacher and asked whether she would like the children to be photographed at Hallowe'en in their wee costumes. She was a bit taken aback to be told that the nursery wasn't celebrating Hallowe'en that year, and asked why. The head teacher said: 'It's the dooking for apples. It's too big a temptation for the staff just to hold some of the kids' heads under until they drown.'

A young child asked his mother: 'Do all fairytales begin with "once upon a time"?' 'No son,' she told him. 'Sometimes they begin with "I'll be working late at the office tonight".'

Reader Nigel Manuel contacts us from New York after our story about the schoolboy whose essay on the funniest thing he ever saw consisted of: 'The funniest thing I ever saw was too funny for words.' Nigel tells us of the pupil at Heatheryknowe Primary School in East Kilbride who had been told to write an essay about a sporting event that they had witnessed. He wrote a title: 'The Cricket Match.' Then below it: 'Rain stopped play.' His teacher, with that unique Scottish sense of humour, rewarded him with two of the belt.

☆ ☆ ☆

Our series of extremely short school essays reminded an East Kilbride teacher of when he set an English prelim for pupils in Glasgow's East End in the mid-1980s. He tells us: 'As usual, there was a candidate who attempted to answer all the essay titles in the time allowed, as opposed to choosing just one from the wide selection provided. One of the titles was: "Glasgow's Miles Better – Do You Agree?" The candidate's pithy answer, as she swept by en route to her next mini-essay, was, in full, "Glasgow may be better, but no' by miles." She was, of course, right, but it was not perhaps what former Lord Provost Michael Kelly would have wanted to hear.'

☆ ☆ ☆

From the general direction of Coatbridge comes a tale of life in the classroom. Teacher is instructing the little ones about collective nouns. You know the kind of thing – a gaggle of geese, a flock of sheep, a celebration of Celtic supporters. The pupils then have to fill in the blanks in a worksheet. They do very well, except for an example to which many give the answer 'a bottle of bells'. This is presumably an insight into the lifestyles of the parents, although legend has it that a certain tonic wine is the libation of choice in those parts.

A young girl, needing help with a school essay, asks: 'Mummy, how did I get here?' Her mother, flustered, falls back on the reliable stork story. 'Oh, I see,' says the little girl, 'and what about you?' The mother assures her that the stork had brought her to Granny as well, a long time ago. The little girl decides to seek a second opinion and goes off to find her grandmother in the next room. 'Granny, how did you get here?' This time, the grandmother tells her that she fell out of a gooseberry bush and her mother had just picked her up while out walking one morning. The little girl shrugs, sits down at her desk and writes: 'As far as I can make out, there hasn't been a natural birth in my family for three generations . . .'

Parents can be so cruel. We are told of the father returning home after a hard day's work and being less than sympathetic when his young son starts his violin practice and the family dog starts howling along with it. 'For goodness' sake,' snapped the father, 'can you not play something the dog doesn't know?'

Lothian's finest were doing their best when they found a group of 14 Italian youths who could not find their lodgings in Edinburgh. So, at four in the morning, the polis phoned the organiser of the Millennium

Commonwealth Youth Games, which were taking place in Edinburgh and asked if the Italians were perhaps lost performers. When the organiser came to, he gently pointed out to the officer that as far as he knew Italy was never actually a member of the British Commonwealth, and went back to sleep.

Our recent tales of children embarrassing their parents reminded Neil Megahy of his granddaughter, while in Primary One, asking her father at Easter: 'Daddy, how do you make love?' Recalls Neil: 'Heart pounding, he had the presence of mind to ask why she wanted to know. "Well," she said, "I know it begins with L". She was sending an Easter card to us.'

We asked for tales of dealing with your children in unorthodox ways. Wilma Malcolm tells us: 'I didn't let on to my son when it was his fourth birthday. We were flitting that day and I just couldn't stand the thought of any more hassle. Now, some 25 years

on, I reckon he's just about forgiven me.' And Irene Foster of Hamilton tells us the sneaky tale: 'When my children were at the toddler stage I ensured a good night's sleep by informing them that "Mummy can't hear in the dark". This strategy ensured that they shouted for Daddy. The poor soul thought for years that he was their very favourite and nobody made him any the wiser.' However, we should mention the cautionary tale from a Glasgow lawyer who tells us of a male friend who was told that the best way to avoid ever having to change the little darling's nappies again was to 'inadvertently' put one on inside out with the shiny side to the bottom so that it would leak. The chap little reckoned on his wife, who, once the baby had erupted to predictable effect, picked him up by the few remaining untarnished areas, carried him down to the shop where he worked, placed him down on the counter in front of suitably offended customers, advised her spouse that it was his expletive fault so he could expletive sort it, then turned on her heel and left.

Various correspondents have given us suggestions of how to divert young offspring when the ice-cream van arrives noisily in the street. Dorothy Bell had a close friend (who cannot be named as he is a high heid yin in social work) who told his poor little girls the chimes they heard on their street were those of a fish van. It was not until they were tall enough to see out of the windows properly that they rumbled him. Ann Ironside of Johnstone says she saved a fortune by telling her weans that the chiming van was there to make sure all the children were in bed. Frank Owens of Baillieston tells of the time his two young sons were misbehaving upstairs. His wife shouted up to them to be quiet. The youngest one bawled back that they would behave if mum gave them both a pound. And his wife replied: 'Why can't you be like your father, and be good for nothing?'

While the Scottish Parliament is attempting to ban smacking weans about the head, some parents use psychological pressure instead. Reader Gordon Anderson was in Clydebank Shopping Centre when he heard a frustrated mother remonstrating with her young charge by shouting: 'If you don't keep quiet, I'm going to have you adopted.' It's being so charming that keeps them going. And a reader overheard the psychological pressure applied in the far more solid middle-class village

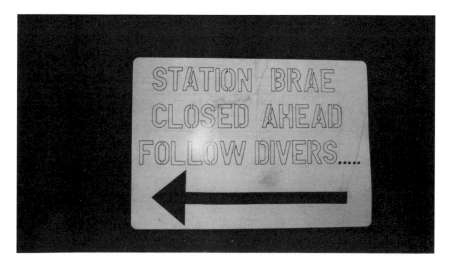

of Cardross, where a harassed woman, trying to get three moppets settled in the car for the morning school run, raised her voice and declared: 'If you don't behave, you'll be going in a taxi.' They can be so cruel, the middle classes.

Seemingly it is not just Scottish mothers who apply psychological pressure to their misbehaving offspring, such as the woman who threatened to have her young one adopted. Ian Miller, now resident in Cambridge, heard a mother there tell her unruly children that she would 'put them back on the at-risk register' if they persisted in their behaviour.

A teacher in Dunbartonshire tells us that the staff were working out what it would be like if the school had a call-centre-type answering service, like BT or Scottish Power. They reckoned the message would be something like this: 'Hello. You have reached the answering service of your child's school. In order to assist you, please listen to all options and make a selection: 'To lie about why your child is absent – press 1. To make excuses for your child not doing his/her homework – press 2. To complain about what we do – press 3. To swear at staff members – press 4. To ask why you did not get important information even though it was in several newsletters and circulars sent to you – press 5. To request another teacher for the third time this year – press 6. To tell us your child is an angel and couldn't possibly have done anything wrong – press 7. If, however, you realise this is the real world and your child must be accountable for his/her own behaviour, classwork and homework, and that it is not the teacher's fault for your child's lack of effort, please hang up, and thanks for calling.'

MURDER POLIS

A chap driving erratically in Glasgow late of a Saturday night is pulled over by the traffic cops, who ask if he's been drinking. 'Well,' he tells them, 'my team won, so I stopped off with my mates for a couple of pints. Then there was a happy hour and they served us some margarita cocktails. And, then, when I dropped my mate off he invited me in for a couple of halfs, and it would have been rude to refuse.' The officer sighs and says: 'I'm afraid you'll have to come to the police car and take a breathalyser test.' 'Why?' says the driver. 'Don't you believe me?'

It is good to see that two English women rescued from Ben Nevis recently only sustained minor injuries. But after reading the statement from Northern Constabulary: 'Sarah Power sustained a groin injury and has been detained in hospital overnight. Sharon Southall sustained a knee injury and, following treatment, was discharged from hospital,' the thought occurs – there wasn't a falling out between the girls, was there?

Attempting to offend as many people as possible, the loud chap in the bar feels he has to tell us: 'Did you hear about the confused Irish police who surrounded a department store in Dublin? Someone had tipped them off

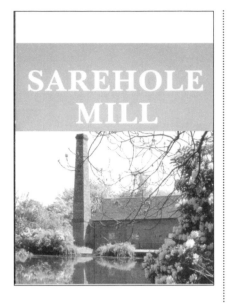

that bed linen was hiding out on the second floor.'

☆ ☆ ☆

We wrote about Greenock Police Station, which reminded a former serving officer there of the sergeant who was nicknamed 'Signal'. He was, apparently, a tube with stripes.

☆ ☆ ☆

As an indication of how tough it has been for the police to gather evidence after the recent drugs-related shootings in Glasgow, one smart-suited chap they stopped said he was a Jehovah's Bystander. When they asked if he did not mean Jehovah's Witness, he told them there were no witnesses around these parts.

☆ ☆ ☆

We are told this is true, and who are we to doubt it? A Glasgow polisman was attending court and read from his notes that 'the accused covered a distance of 30 metres to make the attack'. The defence solicitor, in a sort of Perry Mason mood, challenged him on how accurate he was at estimating distances. So the officer gave as an example his estimate that the court measured 25 metres. The solicitor thought this was too good an opportunity to miss and asked for the court to be measured so that he could show how inaccurate the officer was. However, it was the solicitor who got his comeuppance as the court was measured and it was, indeed, exactly 25 metres long. Everyone was impressed with the constable, and the conviction was assured. Later he told colleagues: 'It was nothing. Before I joined the force I was a joiner and my firm fitted out this building – with twenty-five one-metre ceiling tiles.'

☆ ☆ ☆

We are assured that two Strathclyde traffic police officers pulled over a driver on the M8 for a routine check and, as the officers approached the car, saw the driver smacking his dog, sitting up front with him, on the nose. When they asked him why he was doing that he told them: 'He's a bad dog. He's just eaten my tax disc.'

Further tales of the polis: the locus is Port Glasgow, where two police officers (one male, one female) have occasion to inform a family that their young son is incarcerated at Greenock cop shop. They explain to the father that the presence of a parent would be welcome. The father agrees but asks: 'Is it all right if I go for a single fish first?' The lady polis replies: 'Listen, this is a very serious matter. We haven't got time to stop at a chip shop.'

More polis folklore. A senior officer is on an infrequent patrol in a panda car with a young constable. The pair come across an affray at their locus. They decide that assistance is required. Anxious to be helpful, the senior

We hear of the chap frantically phoning 999 and blurting out that he needs help as his wife has gone into labour and the contractions are only five minutes apart. 'Is this her first child?' the operator asks, trying to be helpful. 'Don't be an idiot,' he shouts back. 'Of course it isn't. It's her husband.'

Glasgow humour – does it travel? We only ask because a Highland police officer tells us about paying a courtesy call on the local duke with a fellow officer who had spent many years in Glasgow. Outside the castle, the duke's nephew is vacuuming out a Land-Rover, and seeing the officers says: 'I say, constable, have you seen my little brother?' 'Naw,' says the Glasgow chap without breaking stride, 'but there's a big lump in your Hoover bag.' The puzzled youth is left staring at his vacuum cleaner.

officer volunteers to radio for help. He picks up the microphone and, searching for the radio call sign, spots a piece of paper stuck on the dashboard above the radio. He intones: 'Foxtrot 32, Romeo 34 to control . . .' The young constable interrupts: 'Chief, you've just read out the tyre pressures.'

☆ ☆ ☆

We are told that in the control room at Paisley police headquarters, a female officer, fed up with the poor reception as she tried to contact officers in the town by radio, was heard to say in a loud voice: 'What do you have to do to get a good roger around here?'

☆ ☆ ☆

In this hi-tech world we were warmed by a low-tech story from William Hutcheson of Paisley. He noted on Teletext that Bath Street in Glasgow was closed due to roadworks. Telephoning police headquarters in Glasgow to check, he was put through to an officer who told him: 'I don't know. I'm in an office in West Regent Street – just a minute and I'll look out the window.' There was a pause, before he came back to say: 'I can see the junction of Bath Street and Holland Street and the traffic is definitely moving.' Ah, who needs CCTV after all?

FORTYSOMETHINGS

What is it like returning to the party scene? Ask fortysomethings with trepidation, their children now old enough to look after themselves, and no excuse now for staying in of a Saturday evening. How has the etiquette of party-going changed since their student days, they inquire anxiously? For a start they no longer need to hide their carry-outs behind the sofa in the front room. The days of concealing your cans of Guinness in case some tightwad who brought only Falcon lager guzzles them instead have now gone. Fortysomethings now have credit cards instead of hard cash, and usually manage a quick sweep through Oddbins before arriving on the doorstep, so you can happily put your booze in the kitchen in full view without putting a padlock on the plastic bag. There may be a couple of wine aficionados there, so avoid taking the bottle of Hungarian Bulls Blood that seemed to hit the spot when you were 17. Most other things will do as long as the label does not say: 'Specially bottled for Safeway.' Remember, 'Tafelwein' is a warning, not a recommendation.

Check, of course, what kind of party it is. Don't make the faux pas of going for a curry and strolling into the party at 11 p.m., unaware that it was in fact a dinner party, and the eight o'clock onwards was not such a lax timetable as you thought. You will be ushered to your seat as the party-giver, with a fixed smile, brings a congealing plateful out of the oven that they have kept for you, as you bluster some far-fetched excuse about being flagged down by a pregnant woman whom you had to take to hospital as police outriders showed the way. Equally, don't go on an empty stomach if the host has invited you to that West End phenomenon, the 'drinks and nibbles' afternoon event, which is an attempt at sophistication, and involves trays of expensive morsels from Marks & Spencer which would barely fill a mouse's belly. You are then in danger of meeting that other phenomenon, the drinking-on-an-empty-stomach sensation which involves you trying to dance the Macarena while everyone else is still discussing Scottish Ballet's latest funding crisis.

There are, of course, plus points about fortysomething parties: for example there is usually no queue at the toilet. This is for two reasons: first, your friends have now traded up the housing ladder so that they have at least two loos and, second, the toilet is no longer clogged with a weeping woman on the toilet seat being comforted by her friends telling her that her boyfriend, now playing tonsil-hockey with someone's younger sister in the kitchen, is a bastard. Fortysomething women have known for years that all men are bastards, and no longer need to sit in the loo for hours reaching that conclusion.

Oh, and if you are waiting to go in the toilet, and a couple come out together, don't leer at them and shout: 'I know what you've been doing.' The sad truth is that she will have dragged him in to show him the complicated shelf arrangement over the bath, and to tell him they should have something similar fitted when they redecorate. Fortysomethings are more likely to run their hands over carpentry than corsetry these days. That's another reason why you should not hark back to your younger days and suggest putting the lights out and playing postman's knock. Mention postman's knock and most folk will assume you are discussing your postal worker's inability to use the door entry security system properly.

Oh, but conversations may be easier. The old maxim of never discussing football or politics no longer applies. Footie is now internationally trendy, so all you have to remember is some Italian-sounding name and suggest Rangers or Celtic are about to sign him. Failing that, you can always try: 'Brazil, how do they learn these skills?' as a conversation starter. Politics couldn't be simpler. Everyone just has a go at New Labour. That has the advantage of hiding whether you are a rabid Red Clydesider or a hoary old Tory, as you can both agree on New Labour's supposed sell-out. In fact, since you last appeared on the party scene, you've probably gone from being a Red Clydesider to an old Tory, so having a common enemy covers the tracks of your embarrassing political journey. Don't worry, there won't be any New Labour people there. They are still out trying to win a seat for Holyrood or Westminster, and don't have time for parties.

You have to be careful about the music, though. There will be some mellow sounds from the Lighthouse Family, or some such, providing the background noise. What you are not supposed to do is find the cupboard drawer full of the old LPs, and remind the hostess of when she declared undying love for David Cassidy. And to show the host his old Deep Purple tracks will only send him into deep brooding about the head of hair he used to assume would be with him for a lifetime. One thing you will notice that's missing is ashtrays. Filling the front room with a fug that Jack the Ripper would feel at home in is no longer acceptable. Instead, you'll be sneaking out of the back door for a fly puff – which is, of course, what you did all those decades ago when you were 14. Funny how what goes around comes around.

THERE was festive fun all round for senior citizens at the annual cabaret organised by Paisley funeral directors J & W Goudie.

Top entertainers Steve Bishop and

WUMMIN

Friends can be particularly cutting. We give as evidence the two women having a conversation in a Glasgow West End bar. One of them is explaining in astonished terms that the Asian girl she works beside is going through with an arranged marriage to a chap she barely knows. Personally speaking, the girl telling the tale is not too keen on the idea, and ends her tirade by saying to her drinking companion: 'Imagine sleeping with a man you've just met!' Her pal swiftly replied: 'I don't know. You seem to do it most Friday nights.' But that's friends for you.

We are told of the woman, unlucky in love, who was adamantly telling her friends that as she had been without a man for a while, she was beginning to think she could easily do without. So one pal mused: 'Oh you'll get your desire back when you meet the right man. After all, there are a number of mechanical devices which increase sexual arousal in women. For example, there is the Mercedes-Benz 380SL convertible.'

We are not ones to add to the arid debate about women drivers, we merely pass on the tale from a Glasgow driving instructor this week who was telling his female pupil to drive up to a roundabout and take the second exit. Once on the roundabout, though, she had forgotten where to go, and she asked: 'Where to?' Seeing a pick-up truck in front with the large letters TOYOTA across the back which was taking the same exit, he told her: 'Just follow the Toyota,' but the exasperated lady told him: 'I'm not an expert on cars. I don't know what a Toyota looks like.'

A woman in Edinburgh at the weekend had the happy glow of pregnancy about her, and an obvious bump. A woman she was introduced to, who was wearing a tight dress with, it has to be said, a bit of a tummy herself, tells the pregnant woman: 'People often think I'm pregnant. But it was lager that did this to me.' The pregnant women replied: 'Do you know, in a funny way lager did this to me as well.'

Telephone folk BT are sending out letters detailing new services from a chap described as the Director of Customer Relationships, which sounds altogether a bit too personal. But

then we overhear two women discussing a service called 1471 erasure, whereby if you dial 1475 after someone has telephoned you, it stops anyone else dialling 1471 to find out who the last caller was. We know that sounds a bit too technical, but it's just that one of the women in the bar described the service as '1475 fancy-man deletion'.

We watched two women have what seemed like a very serious conversation in a Glasgow West End coffee shop until one stopped talking, presumably to draw breath, then told her pal: 'I hate to spread gossip, but what else can you do with it?'

A true story of a woman in Glasgow who was nervous about a rare visit to her house by the minister as she feared her family might not mind their Ps and Qs And because of her nervousness she got a bit mixed up herself, and told the minister that her troublesome son 'did not know his arse from his you-know-what'.

A chap in an office notices an attractive woman who has joined the staff and, after a couple of weeks of general chit-chat at the coffee machine, he asks her out, but she declines. 'This may sound rather old fashioned in this day and age, but I'm keeping myself pure until I meet the man I love,' she tells him. 'That must be a bit of a strain,' the chap replies. 'Oh, I don't mind too much,' she tells him. 'But it has upset my husband quite a bit.'

☆ ☆ ☆

Not every unmarried career woman in her late 30s is desperate for kids, we discover, after overhearing a couple of said types sharing a bottle of South Australian riesling in a West End bar. They were discussing a mutual friend who had children, and one said a bit too loud: 'I visited Christine and her two little darlings last week. By the end of the afternoon my fallopian tubes had voluntarily tied themselves in a knot.'

☆ ☆ ☆

Also showing the spirit of Christmas was the woman in Kilmarnock out with her son, aged about seven. He is staring in a shop window and

excitedly shouts: 'Ma, can I get that for ma Christmas?' Without even turning round to see the object of desire, she tells him: 'Sure, son. Get a job.'

☆ ☆ ☆

Somehow the rumour got around that a good chat-up line is to ask a woman what star sign she is, as it is a female trait to read horoscopes. So we were impressed by the young woman in a Glasgow pub on Christmas Eve, approached by a chap who had clearly stumbled in from a party, who slurred: 'Hey gorgeous, what's your sign?' With a barely perceptible glance at him, she replied: 'Do not enter.'

☆ ☆ ☆

We thought this was an 'only in the West End' story when we heard one Glasgow lady, sharing a bottle of wine – and her worries – in a G12 bar with a male friend, suddenly announce: 'I think my Karma is leaking.' 'Wow,' he said, 'that might be the cause of your problems.' Naturally we shook our heads with that 'we've heard it all now' look. But apparently not. Sanity was restored when she rummaged around in her handbag and said that she had a perfume called Karma, and she thought the top was loose.

☆ ☆ ☆

The curse of modern living. A female reader tells us about the conversation she had in Glasgow's Buchanan Galleries

toilets recently. Settling down on the loo-seat, she was a little surprised to hear a voice from the next cubicle saying: 'Hello?' Not wishing to appear aloof, she replied: 'Hello.' 'Hiya, how ya doing?' said the voice. 'Not bad, thanks,' said the woman. The voice next door sounded a bit put out and continued: 'Hold on a minute . . . do you mind? I'm on the phone . . .'

We pass on the true story of three sisters with the family name Wild who made a pact that as there were no brothers, they would preserve the family name by including it as part of a double-barrelled surname with their spouses. Unfortunately eldest sister Sadie got cold feet when she became engaged to a Joseph Hoare, as she balked at introducing herself as a Wild-Hoare. The other sisters are now avoiding anyone called West, Oates, Rice, or the very unlikely, admittedly, Life-on-one.

Further news on the filming of *Taggart* on the mean streets of Glasgow. At a city-centre location a wee wumman approaches one of the many film people standing about with his walkie-talkie. 'Whit is it ye're daein', son?' she naturally inquires. 'We're filming an episode of *Taggart*,' he politely explains. 'Oh, aye. *Taggart*, eh? Is it a repeat?' she asks.

A woman goes to the personal trainer at the gym and asks: 'Can you teach me to do the splits?' The instructor asks: 'How flexible are you?' So the eager learner tells him: 'I can't make Tuesdays.'

Ladies with hair of a blonde disposition who work for Dumfries and Galloway Council are fed up with the remarks being made about them when they pass on the council's website address. It is dumgal. gov.uk.

Four BBC females were sharing an end-of-week bottle of chenin blanc in Glasgow's West End when one of them announced to her colleagues: 'I saw this magazine article which said that typical symptoms of stress are eating too much, impulse buying, and driving too fast. What are they on about? That sounds like a perfect day to me.'

Ah, the cheery banter of Glasgow. We hear of a chap buying a yum-yum – a twisted piece of sugar-covered pastry, if you must know – in Byres Road, and the young shop assistant was having difficulty with a pair of tongs in picking it up and depositing it inside a paper bag. After at least six attempts to force it into the bag a wee woman in the queue shouted out: 'Just as well you're no' a midwife, hen.' This startled the assistant so much she dropped the offending pastry to the floor, which prompted a further

outburst of: 'Aye, that's right. Drop the poor wee thing oan its heid.'

It was one of these conversations on the Helensburgh to Glasgow train that you can't help being drawn to when a woman was complaining long and loud to her female friend about her marriage. Trying to be supportive, her pal says: 'Yes, I suppose the magic just isn't there after a while,' to which her dispirited friend snapped back: 'Oh there's still some magic. Every Saturday night he disappears.'

The recently wed wife turned to her husband in their spick-and-span house in the Mearns, gently held his hand, and quietly told him: 'I've got great news. There's going to be three of us in the house soon instead of two.' Her husband was almost speechless with emotion, and kissing his wife said: 'You've made me the happiest man in the world.' A relieved wife told him: 'I'm so glad. To be honest I didn't think you'd take it so well when I told you my mother was moving in with us.'

> **WILD** cat, mounted and stuffed by Lord Gainford, Taynish Estate, glass case, slightly cracked, £5.

A young Glasgow chap has eventually met the girl of his dreams and tells his folks he is going to get married. But, just to tease his mother, he says he is bringing three women over for dinner, and she has to guess which one is his intended. When the three girls are seated at the table, he follows his mum into the kitchen and asks her excitedly which one she thinks it is. 'The one in the middle,' his mother says without hesitation. 'That's right. How did you know?' he asks. 'I don't like her,' says his mother.

We pass on the comments of a young lady who turned up at Barlinnie Prison in Glasgow to visit her man, only to find a strike disrupting visiting times. Angrily pointing at the striking prison officers, she declared: 'If it wisnae fur ma man, they widnae huv an effan joab.' But the officers themselves are not without a sense of mirth. When another agitated lady declared that their actions were stopping her man from being released that morning, one officer was heard to mutter under his breath: 'It was her man who organised the strike so he wouldn't have to see her coupon this morning.'

The scene is a butcher's shop in Pollokshields where a wee Govan wumman has paused to purchase a ham end. She would normally have

Lisa Presley engagement off

The engagement between Lisa Maria Presley and Nicholas Cage is over.

A joint statement from the couple said yesterday that they ended a 10-month relationship a fortnight ago, but "hoped to remain friendly".

Lisa, 33, heiress to Elvis Presley's £100 million fortune, met the 37-year-old star of *Captain Corelli's Mandolin* at a Los Angeles party.

Lisa Maria Presley

bought it at her local shop but had been visiting relatives in Pollokshields and found herself in these slightly more upmarket premises. The butcher duly wrapped up her bit of ham and asked for a sum of money adjacent to £2. The Govan lady, used to paying something closer to 50p, said: 'No thanks, son, it's for making soup, no for ma display cabinet.'

☆ ☆ ☆

A group of young professional women in Glasgow, easing their way into the weekend with chardonnay, are discussing the best way to get rid of any creeps who come up and pester them in the street. They were reaching the conclusion that, rather than humour them, you should just say very loudly: 'Go away or I will call the police.' One of their number, who had been very quiet until then, blurted out an alternative: 'I usually find that saying "I love you and want to marry you and have your children" gets rid of men very quickly.'

☆ ☆ ☆

Travelling can be so stressful at times, so one can forgive the woman – a nurse at a major Glasgow hospital, apropos of nothing – who got quite flustered racing for her train across the width of Central Station, and ended up startling the crowds coming in the opposite direction, by shouting 'Gangbang, gangbang' as she tried to clear a path to her train.

A very roundabout compliment is overheard in a Glasgow department store where an ample lady had just bought a suitably ample blouse. While wrapping it up, the size-ten assistant gushed: 'I love this blouse. I just wish I was fat enough to wear it.'

We are told of a group of high-spirited nurses being given a guided tour of a Glasgow fire station where part of the tour featured a demonstration of the infrared thermal imaging camera, used to detect hot-spots in smoke-filled buildings. The firefighters thought it would be funny to heat up a few large bananas in a microwave oven and conceal them in their waterproofs shortly before the demonstration took place. One by one the nurses had a long, meaningful squint through the camera's eye piece before silently handing it over to her colleague next in line. Needless to say the chaps didn't crack a light about their prank, and have now been inundated by requests for the tour to become a regular feature on the nurses' social calendar.

A woman was shocked when her grandmother told her that her grandfather died of a heart attack while making love. When the young woman expressed surprise, her grandmother said: 'Oh yes, we had sex every Sunday morning in time with the church bells. In fact,' she added, wiping away a tear, 'if it hadn't been for that blasted ice-cream van he might still be with us.'

An Ayrshire lady was pointing out to a chap the Mir space station, which was visible as a bright star-type light in the sky. Clearly not grasping the concept, he remarked that it must be some size of light that they had left on if you could see it so far away.

Sadly, there are still men out there who overindulge at the New Year. We hear of one such chap tottering home just before dawn with booze on his breath and lipstick on his collar. His naturally angry wife greeted him with: 'I assume there is a very good reason for you to come waltzing in here at six o'clock in the morning?' Foolishly he tried the jocular reply: 'There is. Breakfast.'

A Lenzie woman woke up the other day and enthusiastically told her husband: 'I just dreamed that you gave me a diamond necklace as a New Year's gift.' Coyly she added: 'What do you think it means?' 'Well, you'll know tonight,' he tells her. True enough, that evening he came home with a small package which he presented to her. Delighted, she tore it open – to find a book entitled *The Meaning of Dreams*.

The cashier in the busy department store couldn't help noticing that a woman customer rummaging in her bag for her purse brought out a television remote control. She couldn't help herself, and had to ask the shopper why she was carrying it. 'Because my husband refused to come shopping with me, and I smile every time I think of him trying to cope without it.'

A concerned husband was talking to his doctor pal. 'My wife has lost her voice. What can I do to help her get it back?' His pal tells him: 'Try coming home at three in the morning.'

Domestic violence should never be condoned, but we hear of the frail old chap, giving evidence in court against his wife, who claimed that she hit him with a maple leaf. 'Surely that couldn't have caused you any serious injury?' inquired the defence lawyer. 'It does when it's the leaf from the centre of the dining room table,' the old chap explained.

Chardonnay, as we have pointed out before, has been the downfall of many a Glasgow West End woman on a night out. We pass on the tale of the young woman imbibing too much in Ashton Lane who keeled over backwards in a bar, and was caught by a startled chap standing behind her. To give her credit though, she gathered up her dignity, and told her shiny armoured knight: 'I like a man who can hold his drunk.'

A few friends who had met up in Hyndland in Glasgow's West End had sloshed back a couple of bottles when the hostess teetered off to her loo. There, she espied her fancy, expensive soaps on display in a wicker basket, and decided to try one. On her return to the lounge she expressed her disappointment at its lack of lather and perfume. It was a friend who next went to the loo, and noticed that the cellophane was still on the bar.

Women who lunch in Newton Mearns fear a new deadly virus called MAIDS. Apparently they would just die if they didn't have a little woman who came in twice a week for a little light dusting and cleaning.

Two women in the doctor's surgery were fussing around a new mother with triplets who went in to the doc's for a post-natal check-up. When the mother left the waiting room one woman remarked: 'I read somewhere that it is one chance in 12,000 that you have triplets.' 'Goodness,' said the other woman. 'How did she ever find the time to do any housework?'

We hear of the Scots woman travelling in continental Europe who discovers that she has to share a sleeping carriage with a man she has never met. After the initial embarrassment, the man takes the top bunk, but in the middle of the night leans down, wakes her up, and says: 'I'm very cold, can you get me another blanket from somewhere?'

Coming to, she tells him: 'I've got a better idea. Let's pretend we're married.' 'That's a great idea,' blurts out the chap, thinking Christmas had arrived early. 'Good,' said the woman. 'Get your own bloody blanket.'

A couple discussing Posh's attempt at modelling in scanty outfits. Said one: 'Did you see her arse?' 'Aye,' replied the pal, 'he was sitting in the front row wearing a bandana.'

A chap gets fed up with his wife complaining about the amount of time he spends in the pub, so he eventually invites her along. Once inside, he asks her what she wants, and she replies: 'Oh, I don't know. The same as you, I suppose.' He orders two whiskies and downs his in a gulp, and his wife emulates him. At that she splutters, screws her face up and tells him: 'I don't know how you can drink this stuff.' 'There you go,' he tells her. 'And you thought I was out enjoying myself every night.'

WUMMIN

A wife was watching her husband standing on the bathroom scales, sucking in his stomach. Thinking it was a pathetic attempt to weigh less, she told him: 'I don't think that is going to help.' 'It will,' he grumpily told her. 'It's the only way I can see the numbers.'

An agitated young woman, possibly from the Home Counties, is telling a young man in the Café Royal in Edinburgh about an accident she had in her Mazda MX5. 'So the chap just ran straight into the back of me, and I ran into the taxi in front,' she moaned. The chap in the unstructured suit nods, clucks compassionately, and asks: 'What gear were you in?' With a puzzled frown she racks her memory before telling him: 'Umm, Gucci slacks and a turquoise pashmina.'

As the two women shared a bottle of the wine of the month in a West End bar, one was heard to moan: 'I'm so fed up with men and their fear of commitment.' 'You're telling me,' says her pal. 'I had to say to John that after going out together for a year and a half I had to give him an ultimatum.' 'What did you say?' said the friend now draining the bottle of rough Sicilian. 'Well I just told him straight. "Either you tell me your surname or it's over."'

BATMAN AND ROBBIN'

A rep for a drinks company based in Edinburgh is a tad nervous about visiting a bar in Glasgow's Possil housing scheme. It's not the most salubrious, it has to be said, and when he walks in all heads turn and you could hear a pin drop. After chatting to the owner he offers to bring him some branded optics and ashtrays in from his car and steps outside. At that he notices two very bulky menacing chaps follow him out, so he quickly dives into the Co-op next door, where he nervously tells staff he is doing a price comparison on whiskies while watching the two heavies look up and down the street. Eventually, after quarter-of-an-hour, he goes outside, and, with no sign of the lads, nips to his car, gets the goods, and takes them back into the pub, hoping his unease isn't showing. 'Where did you get to?' said the owner. 'I sent Jim and Archie there to look after you, but they said you disappeared.'

Strange how language changes. A true story from a Glasgow call centre that takes breakdown phone calls for a motoring organisation. The caller says his car is damaged 'after running over a small dyke'. Without thinking, the girl taking the call says: 'Is she OK?'

Of course, being a West of Scotland mother makes you particularly defensive about your sons. We are told of the mum waiting at the test centre while her son was sitting his driving test. She could see from his glum expression that he had failed, so she asked the examiner what went wrong. The examiner said her son had failed to stop at a red light. 'Well,' persisted the lad's mother, 'just how red was the light?'

☆ ☆ ☆

Ian Deuchar of Milngavie told us of the insensitive chap who went up to a *Big Issue* seller and said: 'Knock knock.' When the street vendor, in the hope of a sale, replied: 'Who's there?' his tormentor sneered: 'Oh, so you've

got a hoose then' and walked on.

☆ ☆ ☆

Spotted in a shop window in Perth, perhaps placed by a disgruntled spouse: 'Abdominal exerciser for sale, very good condition, hardly used, £15.' There then followed a phone number and the telling phrase: 'Ask for Fatty.'

☆ ☆ ☆

Dipping once again into nicknames, Tom O'Hagan, a former teacher in Glenlivet, tells us that in the distillery community there was a chap called Mothie. Apparently when he was out on the batter he never wanted to call it a night, so would turn up at any house where he saw a light on.

☆ ☆ ☆

BBC news presenter Jane Franchi was a tad nervous before replying on behalf of the lassies at David Sole's charity Burns supper in Edinburgh. As she explained to the 400 guests: 'I normally present *Newsnight Scotland* and *Good Morning Scotland*, so you are without doubt the biggest audience I have ever had.' She also delighted the women by declaring: 'Is my husband hard to please? I haven't the faintest idea.' And as for fellow BBC presenter, the comfortably built Tam Cowan, she explained: 'Tam is leaving his body to medical science when he dies. Medical science is contesting the will.'

Our neighbours, Scottish Television, take complaints from viewers very seriously, and even have comment forms which are methodically filled out by the inquiries department and circulated to the bosses. We sneaked a look at one such form which we feel should have wider circulation – possibly because we fear we may identify too much with said complainer. It states: 'After some time on the phone I discovered that the problem was that the viewer's remote control had stopped working. He didn't believe that it took batteries, and thinks that our service is unsatisfactory as we were unwilling to post him out a new remote control. (He will be in touch with the newspapers about this.)'

A well-known Scottish tenor who has attended Burns suppers in the exotic climes of Egypt tells us the locals there have their own name for today's celebration – it's known as The Feast of Ramadram.

As usually happens, our occasional mention of unusual nicknames produced the surreal claim that a chap in Bathgate who was a paratrooper during the war lost vital bits of his anatomy when he landed on a mine in Belgium. His surname is Steele. His nickname is allegedly Stainless. And the docker known as Batman – apparently he couldn't leave the docks without Robin.

A soprano in Edinburgh was waiting in for a joiner. Since the doorbell didn't always work, she had taped below it a sign saying 'Bell Temperamental'. The joiner, when he finally arrived, was fascinated by her tales of being a diva. When the job was done he handed over the invoice, announcing that he would treasure the signature on the cheque, but on inspecting it looked disappointed. It was then that she noticed that the invoice had been made out to Miss Belle Temperamental.

Dipping once again into nicknames, we hear of the chap called Genie. Apparently, if you took a cork out of a bottle he would be at your side in seconds.

We are trying to identify the street in Glasgow where we are told there is resentment caused by a chap claiming disability benefits, although apparently as able-bodied as the next man. It gets even worse when the council paints a white box outside his house with the word DISABLED on it so that he can park his car without hindrance. Finally a neighbour, during the night, paints over the two Ds in the word in order to make a point. But the gesture is lost on the wife of the dodgy claimant who expresses her incredulity to neighbours by telling them: 'There's nobody in this house called Isabel,' thus adding poor spelling to their list of crimes.

Ever since *The Herald* moved up town to Cowcaddens we have not been in Babbity Bowster as often as we would like, so we have not been able to check the following tale told to us by a regular at the friendly hostelry. He tells us: 'One day at the Babbity a guy stuck his head in and asked the proprietor, Fraser Lawrie: "Do you mind if I bring in a bunch of guys I've got with me?" "That depends," said Fraser. "Are they good boys or will they cause any bother?" "No really, it's just that they are a blind football team." Now Fraser is intrigued and asks how they play football if they are blind, but the chap explains it really isn't that difficult as they put some bells

inside the ball and they know where it is by the sound of the jingling. At this point another guy came rushing into the bar and disturbed the conversation by asking: "Who's in charge of that bunch of guys from the minibus?" "Me," said the prospective customer, "why?" "Well you better come quick – they're kicking the hell out of a couple of Morris dancers out there".'

An Ayrshire chap was describing the circumstances in which he had failed his driving test. The examiner had asked him if he could remember the first sign he had seen on leaving the test centre. 'Yes,' replied our eager candidate, 'it was "Strawberries £2 a punnet".'

Oor bar-room philosopher tells us that God must be a man. Warily we ask why. 'Because if God was a woman, after she said "Let there be light" she would say "Hmm. Let me see the dark again."'

FOOTBALL CRAZIES

Duncan Ferguson is a great footballer for Everton, although he may not be in the queue to join Mensa. That said, it is surely cruel that someone in the know swears on a stack of Bibles that Duncan telephoned the company that put a new security system in his house to say he did not know the code for switching off the alarm. The woman at the other end began to explain: 'They just use the standard code of 1-2-3-4 until you decide on your own,' but was interrupted by Duncan who said: 'Hang on while I get a pen.'

Rangers fans are getting their sense of humour back, even if some of it will no doubt be dismissed as politically incorrect. A consular official who attended the Rangers tie against Fenerbahce in Turkey, where the local fans like to parade banners stating 'Welcome to Hell', tells us he winced a bit when he saw a very small group of Rangers fans at the match who unveiled a banner which declared: 'If you think this is Hell, wait till you get to Sighthill.'

Scotland's footballing traditions are being kept alive on the other side of the world, we hear. Gary Johnson of Byron Bay in New South Wales tells

us of his local football team which was a man short last week, so the lads asked in the local backpacker hostel if anyone wanted to play. Up came a chap who described himself as 'Thomas frae Cumnock', and to show off his footballing credentials claimed he was related to Roy Aitken, the former Celtic favourite. It appears Oor Tam showed many of his relative's silky skills by going over the top in a tackle in the first move, which led to him being booked by the ref. In the ensuing discussion Tam was less than complimentary to the ref and a red card was produced – quite possibly Byron Bay's quickest ordering off. Well done, Thomas, in keeping up Scotland's footballing name.

☆ ☆ ☆

The sights you see in the morning. It is still quite dark early on and a chap who runs to work through Erskine jogs across the local football pitches. He sees the goalposts ahead of him through the gloom and sprints towards them, imagining no doubt that they are the finishing posts at the London Marathon. Just as he surges through the goal he finds himself on his back, struggling even to get to his feet. Yes, the nets had not been taken down from the game of football the day before, and he is trussed up like a bag of oranges, much to the amusement of passers-by. See, we always knew this exercise lark was a dangerous thing.

☆ ☆ ☆

Partick Thistle manager John Lambie, the Mr Malaprop of Maryhill, could opt for the literary route if he wanted a change of career, by writing his life story. The thrills would involve one chapter devoted to Lambieisms:

> We shot ourselves in the arm.
> We didn't bury them off.
> We knew they would come

out for the second half with all guns running.

I'm away home to put my head in my birthday cake – the cake's in the oven.

These Lambieisms reminded Stewart Richardson, of Baillieston, of the time the great man was interviewed on the radio and was asked about the excellent winning goal. John replied: 'Aye, the boy took it well, it was a textstyle finish.' Recalls Stewart: 'Funnily enough, Texstyle World was the Thistle shirt sponsor at the time, so maybe it was a clever marketing ploy rather than a faux pas.'

The sayings of John Lambie are not merely malapropisms and other slips of the tongue. He employs a rich and colourful language to paint verbal pictures. When radio commentator Charlie Mann on Sportsound asked him, after Thistle won despite losing three goals, if his defence was giving him cause for concern, John told him: 'Defenders! They're no bloody defenders – they couldnae keep weans oot a bloody close.' And exuding an almost Zen aura, he told commentator Ken McRobb, who asked him if it was going to be easy after Thistle had opened up a considerable lead in the League: 'Ah well, Ken, it's like this, it's a long, long road that disnae have a turn.'

Celtic star bhoy Neil Lennon is asked to leave a Glasgow club after brawling with another patron, one of the tabloids reports. It reminds us of the occasion at Christmas when he skint his face after falling out of a taxi. Another Glasgow taxi driver, possibly of the bluenose variety, swears blind that when Lennon fell out, a top Scots referee who was in the taxi behind, rolled down his window, and immediately awarded a penalty.

Coin-struck Aberdeen player Robbie Winters, quoted on Teletext after some trouble at a game against Rangers: 'It had to be stopped because there was £10 worth of change out there.' And thus the stories of Aberdeen's legendary meanness continue to be fuelled.

A tale from a European tie penalty shoot-out at Celtic Park. As the players lined up for the vital kicks, a group of fans was discussing what to shout at the Valencia players to try to put them off, with one saying: 'We need to shout the Spanish word for "miss".' Raising his voice he inquired: 'Does anybody know the Spanish for miss?' From behind, someone shouted back: 'Senorita.'

Scots continue to find it hard to be understood abroad. Gordon Gosnold in Australia tells us about a Scottish colleague who coaches a mainly Croatian football side in his spare time. The coach met one of his star players while out shopping, and was introduced to the player's wife. He was delighted to meet her, and told her that wives were all too often omitted from club get-togethers, and that this should be changed. He then made his farewells, but the player's wife tensed up and moved a few steps away. When the coach left, the Croatian lady said to her husband: 'Are the Scots always so forward?' And when her husband asked why, she told him: 'What did he mean "we must get together and have a couple of babies some time"?' It was then explained to her that he had actually said they should get together 'for a couple of bevvies' – an honourable tradition, of course, in any language.

Willie Young, one of Scotland's more controversial referees, opened his heart as guest speaker at Prestwick St Nicholas golf club's 150th anniversary dinner. Asked why he donned the reviled black outfit and took up the whistle, he replied: 'I was at the stage where I wasn't enjoying my football – and I didn't see why anyone else should either.' He spoke warmly of ex-Scotland supremo Craig Brown and said that many people didn't know

that Craig got a blue at Oxford. He added that he would also have got a pink if it had not been behind the black.

☆ ☆ ☆

The BBC is threatening to halt television coverage of Celtic games at Parkhead following complaints of rats in among the wiring. The club is no doubt wondering where it can get someone who plays the flute to tempt them away.

☆ ☆ ☆

Sir Alex Ferguson, back up in Glasgow with his Manchester United for the Tom Boyd testimonial, was recalling his last major appearance in Glasgow when he was made Freeman of the City. 'Does that mean you can graze your sheep in George Square?' he was asked by one astute fan who knows that such awards often have archaic attachments. 'No,' said Sir Alex, 'the only useful clause is that if I get lifted I'm entitled to a cell of my own.'

☆ ☆ ☆

Although Motherwell Football Club stayed at home during one SPL winter break, keeper Andy Goram and a few mates managed to fit in a trip to New York. We are assured this is true by a fan who tells us: 'Yes, I saw him at New York airport in the duty-free eyeing up a 16-year-old brandy. But then her parents arrived and took her away.'

We admired former Celtic captain Billy McNeill's mental agility when a reporter from the *Boston Herald* (no relation) visited Glasgow to write a five-day series on Old Firm rivalry, dwelling perhaps a little too much on the violence that can sometimes occur. To quote the *BH*: 'A seemingly innocent act such as passing by a pub wearing a scarf of the wrong colour is to invite what Glaswegians describe as a "claim". Claims are generally settled in hand-to-hand combat, although sometimes the odds are evened by resorting to the city's weapons of choice – a razor or a broken beer bottle.' So you get the idea. Anyway, when the American chap asked Billy about the violence he replied: 'If you want to talk about fighting and knives, I suggest you go speak to the cowboys and Indians.' Anyway, the *BH* has a talk-back page for e-mail messages which included one from an irate Rangers fan who must have confused Bostonians by claiming: 'Has your so-called reporter applied for a job with a so-called newspaper called the *Daily Record*? If not, he should, his article is just about as low as we have come to expect from that rag.' And the sender of such an epistle? 'Sparkie fae Larkie.'

The public house has become the venue where the sport of football is mainly consumed. Yet most pubs have strict rules prohibiting the wearing of football colours. One publican, who shall remain nameless, is particularly rigorous in enforcing this rule. When a customer sporting a scarf of a certain denomination was reluctant to remove said garment, mine host warned: 'Take off that scarf or I'll wrap it round your neck.'

FOOTBALL CRAZIES

A Glaswegian exiled in Edinburgh, Allan Snedden, realised he missed the rhythm of his old city when he returned last week for a football match and found himself queuing for food outside the park. The chap in front asked for chips and curry sauce. As the greeny-yellow goo was poured over the chips, the chap's pal stared at it dubiously, then told his mate: 'That reminds me. I can't go for a pint after the game. Ma dug's no well.'

We are told of the devoted wife who had spent her life taking care of her retired football player husband. But he was now in poor health, slipping in and out of a coma, as she sat every day at his bedside. Coming to, he motioned her to come close, and he whispered to her: 'You've been with me through all the bad times. When I broke my leg you were there to support me. When I got dropped after failing to score for ten games, you were by my side. When I ended up back in the Juniors after my heavy drinking, you were there for me. There's something I have to tell you.' Leaning forward, she gently asked: 'What's that, dear?' He whispered: 'I think you bring me bad luck.'

Lisbon Lion Bobby Lennox was entertaining Durham Celtic Supporters Club recently. He was telling them how sophisticated the equipment in the training room now is. He said the players now eat a far more healthy diet than in his day, and that there were machines that can tell you what you had to eat and drink the night before. 'We had one too,' he told them. 'It was called Jock Stein.'

SEMIOPATHY

We picked up on a word coined by the *New Scientist* to describe signs and phrases which could be open to humorous ambiguity – semiopathy.

Reader Dorothy Bell's favourite concerned a friend who had a large volume of items being posted to her, which proved a nuisance as she had a small letterbox. One day she received a folded-up set of documents labelled: 'Photographs Do Not Bend', to which her postie had added: 'They Do.' John Clough saw a sign at Whitby Harbour in Yorkshire which stated 'Fishing for Children Only'. He wondered if you could fling back ones which proved tiresome as they grew older. And from *The Herald* itself, he said his father was amused by the Glasgow Eye Hospital advertisement for 'Pupil Nurses'.

Reader Ian Petrie told us his favourite advertisement: 'Eat British Beef – You Will Not Get Better.' Iain Smith of Nerston, East Kilbride, recalls a sign in the Trossachs that read 'Sheep keep dogs on lead' which, obviously, they do not. But, as Mr Smith points out, 'Gentlemen lift the seat.'

Glenn Surtees delved into semiopathy with the sign 'Treatment Works' which he saw near Oban. It should give NHS patients a confidence boost. And Paul McGivern was puzzled by a sign in Paisley. 'Slow Children Playing.' Where do the smarter kids go?

Barney Macfarlane of Kames, Tighnabruaich, offered: 'There is a sign on the approach to a local holiday chalet park which says "Watch for Children" which I think is a most generous offer.' Dave Anderson, thespian and music man, is intrigued by a sign in Bar Brel in Ashton Lane, Glasgow, which reads 'This door is unhinged'. Makes a change from doors being alarmed. A number of readers have pointed out the sign north of Dundee which says 'Welcome to Angus', which is OK for him, but what about the rest of us.

John Calderwood of Cardross adds to our investigation by telling us that at Belfast airport the Wheelchair Assembly Point was empty without a single traveller whiling away the waiting time by putting some equipment together.

Gary McCracken opines: 'When approaching roadworks on the dual carriageway outside Falkirk, I followed the roadside instruction to "Use Both Lanes" – apparently to the annoyance of other drivers.'

Iain Carruthers of Erskine points out the sage advice: 'To avoid suffocation, keep away from children.' And Calum MacKinnon wonders how valid is the road sign in Paisley which claims: 'Way Out Town Centre.'

Drummond Small of Kilmaurs recalls relatives in Ireland who had the religious saying 'Jesus Christ, the same today, the same tomorrow, the same forever,' adorning a wall. He often thought it was a rant against boredom.

John Cameron of Drymen tells us: 'I'm always baffled by all those cars with "Baby on board" signs. Why don't they just put them in a car seat?'

☆ ☆ ☆

'"Disabled toilet" – why don't they fix it then?' asks Eddie Rodger of Glasgow. And David Sutherland of Troon wonders why at important meetings there is a sign which says 'Press Table', but when you do, nothing happens.

☆ ☆ ☆

A number of readers say they look at their bottles of still mineral water, and can confirm that every time they check, the contents haven't changed.

☆ ☆ ☆

A reader tells us: 'Seen in a shop window, "Manager's Special". So at least his mother loves him.'

☆ ☆ ☆

Jamie Campbell says: 'Commuting to work the other day, I was delighted to spot the following advertisement: "To drive this bus: £7.25 an hour after one year's service, £6 per hour now." However, on presenting the bus driver with my £6, he seemed somewhat less than willing to hand over control of the vehicle.'

Dave Newbigging tells us: 'Boxes labelled "Fragile This Way Up", so why arrange them that way?'

SCOTTISH HOSPITALITY

Donald Macaskill of Glasgow tells us: 'In a hotel not all that far from Cambridge Street, the company annual dinner was getting under way. At the top table a somewhat imperious lady was going through the fixed menu item by item with the waitress. "And is the beef on the bone?" was delivered with just a touch of the Lady Bracknells. "Aye," responded the young lassie with an impatient toss of her head, "else coos would look like jellyfish."'

Glasgow florist Sandy Martin popped into Tennent's Bar in Byres Road after a round of golf at Gleneagles with two chums who thought Tennent's would be better value than the £5 bacon roll at the Dormie House. Sandy ordered gammon steak with a fried egg, then thought the young barmaid had asked him if he wished a Caesar salad. Warmed by the bar's sophistication he said he would be delighted with a Caesar salad, only for the barmaid to retort: 'This is Tennent's – I said peas or salad.'

In a hotel on the Isle of Arran a hapless Sassenach had the misfortune to ask the ferociously grumpy host for a full English breakfast. One glower

was enough to have the guest stammer that it was a full Scottish breakfast he wanted. As Basil McFawlty was shuffling back to the kitchen, the guest tried to redeem himself by shouting: 'Just one egg for me this morning.' Our man turned and barked: 'Who's been giving you two eggs?'

☆ ☆ ☆

A north-east couple were in New York when they were stopped by a local intrigued by their accents, who asks where they are from. 'We're fae Aberdeen, Scotland,' says the husband, who is interrupted by his hard-of-hearing wife who says: 'Ehh, fits he saying?' so the husband repeats the conversation for her. The New Yorker says he knows Aberdeen and asks which part they are from. 'It's actually Inverurie, just ootside o' Aberdeen', and again the wife says: 'Ehh, fits he saying?' so the husband repeats the conversation. The New Yorker expresses surprise, and says he knows Inverurie well, as it was where he had the worst sexual experience of his life. 'Ehh, fits he saying?' inquires the good lady, to which her husband replies in exasperation: 'He says he kens ye.'

☆ ☆ ☆

A school in Ayrshire, we hear, recently played host to a team of young rugby players from Canada who were farmed out among the various families. One of the Canadians was then taken on a tour of Ayrshire by his host family who pointed out to him Robert Burns' Cottage. Seeing the lack of response, they asked if he knew who Burns was. Alas, the chap answered in the negative. Trying a different tack, they persevered with: 'Have you heard of Auld Lang Syne?' Trying to be helpful, the young Canadian came back with: 'What position does he play in?'

The scene is an Airtours jet bringing holidaymakers back from Malaga to Gatwick. The cabin crew are Scottish. A stewardess asks a question of an English lady who retorts irately: 'How dare you ask me if I've had sex!' The girl, believed to be of Fife origin, explains, possibly in less of a Fife accent: 'No, I asked, have you headsets? You know, for listening to the in-flight entertainment.'

An American searching for his roots on Tiree is chatting to a local about the burial customs on the island, and asks if it is true that the family take the coffin around the homes of friends before the burial. The old fellow, trying to conceal a twinkle in his eye, tells him: 'Yes, indeed. You stop at everyone's home where the family pay their respects to the deceased and pour a dram for the burial party. In some of the houses, of course, the rooms are so small that you have to stand the coffin up on its end. But perhaps too many drams are poured . . .' 'Why's that,' asks the anxious American. 'Because it would explain why so many grandfather clocks have been buried on Tiree,' he adds.

We Scots can be so disparaging of our own kailyard. A reader flying back to Glasgow from the East Midlands yesterday heard an American ask the Scots traveller next to him: 'Do you think I'll find an internet café open in East Kilbride tonight?' His fellow passenger, barely looking up from his newspaper, told him: 'In East Kilbride you'll be lucky to get a phone box that works.'

Further testament to the glorious service offered to visitors to Scotland. A tourist goes into the public bar of a west coast island hotel for a bite to eat. The menu offers soup of the day. He asks the chap behind the bar what kind of soup it is. Potato, he is told, but when it arrives, the reddish hue indicates that it is, in fact, tomato. Naturally the tourist opines: 'I thought you said it was potato soup?' Without a word, his server takes a couple of tatties from another customer's plate, drops them in the soup, and declares, no doubt in Kenneth Wolstenholme tones: 'It is now.' Somewhat taken aback, the tourist asks to see the manager. 'Certainly,' he is told. 'If you go through to reception and ring the bell, the manager will see you.' The ever-so-slightly miffed visitor disappears to find reception. A couple of minutes later a bell rings. The chap who can turn

tomato into potato soup sighs, puts on his jacket, and goes off to deal with whoever is ringing the bell in reception.

A returning holidaymaker tells us of his trip to southern Spain, where he got into conversation with a London chap who informed him that he now lived permanently in Spain. 'So what brought you here?' asks the holidaymaker after they'd shared a libation or two. 'Your job?' 'Yes, mate,' he replies, then adds: 'Well, actually two jobs. One was a bank, the other was a post office.'

The tourist season often brings strange phone calls to the police station at Oban. We are told of a recent call there by a woman in Ireland who wanted to take visitors from America to Iona, and wondered how to get there. The policeman, being in helpful mode, explained that there was no direct route from Ireland, and she would need to take a ferry from Larne to Stranraer, drive up to Oban, take the ferry to Mull,

> **Do you consider yourself the rightful successor to Joan Bakewell as "the thinking man's crumpet"?**
> *John Summers, by e-mail*
> I'm not very keen on crumpets but I love a muffin.

drive down the island, and take the small ferry to Iona. This did not cheer up the woman who, clearly wearying at the thought of it, remarked: 'I don't know why she wants to go to Iona anyway.' The ever-helpful officer told her it was probably because of the historic interest in that Columba had sailed from Ireland to Iona in order to bring Christianity to Scotland. 'Well,' says the caller, 'why can't we take the ferry he used?'

Strange are the conversations of our tourists. A couple are in a tourist information office on Skye, obviously planning the next stage of their Scottish tour. Looking at the racks of leaflets, the chap is heard saying to his partner: 'Have you ever been to Plockton?' She says she doesn't think so, which makes her partner add: 'It's beautiful. It's where they filmed *Hamish Macbeth*.' To which the young lady replied: 'Nah, I don't fancy that. I'm no really into Shakespeare and all that.'

On CalMac's Isle of Mull ferry from Oban, the chap in the café is trying hard to remember his training, and is politely welcoming everyone. 'Good morning, madam. What can I get you?' he asks. The lady requests some toast. His face clouds over. 'Sorry, madam. The toaster's buggered. Would you like a roll?'

RELIGION'S NO JOKE

Religious jokes are an area where we tread carefully. But this is acceptable. Three ministers were discussing ways of ridding their buildings of bats – before they became a protected species, of course. The first says he used a pest control firm at enormous expense, but the bats returned six months later. The second, to economise, got several volunteers up in the rafters with gas bombs, but the bats returned a few weeks later. The third said: 'My way's very cheap. I just baptise them in the church and they never come back.'

Father Jim Lawlor, one of the Catholic chaplains on the ecumenical chaplaincy team at Glasgow's Barlinnie Prison, was visiting a new admission in the Young Remand Unit who was obviously a bit edgy about being so close to a Catholic priest. Jim tells us: 'When trying to put him at ease with small talk, I inquired about his age. "I'll be 17 in 2 weeks," he replied; on my own birthday, in fact. "Oh," I said, "that means we are both Capricorns." "No me, mate," he replied urgently, "I'm a Protestant."'

Someone not clear on the concept. When the news on the pub telly announced Mario Conti as the new archbishop of Glasgow, a voice was heard to mutter: 'Typical. Another top job in Glasgow going to a Catholic. Where will it all end?'

The minister at Glasgow University Chapel's watchnight service, when introducing a well-known carol, said his young daughter had been quite taken by the original printing in the Order of Service which read 'Hark the Herald Angels Sin.' It reminds us of the one that crops up regularly in Scotland of folk who think the seasonal hymn is actually 'A Wean in a Manger'.

Further evidence that the Church of Scotland is now meaning less to the youth of the country. A young woman watching telly recently sees a chap appear on her screen, below him is the caption 'Kirk Moderator'. In all seriousness, she says to her sister: 'That's an unusual name. Do you think he's Canadian?'

Former Bishop of Edinburgh Richard Holloway spoke eloquently to an audience about the trials of religious belief, and explained how he would wake up at four in the morning depressed and wrestling with doubts. So, in that practical way they do so well in Glasgow, when he took questions from the audience a woman asked him: 'This deep depression. Have you checked your blood sugar level? Would a wee digestive biscuit not cheer you up a bit?'

DON'T WHISTLE WHILE YOU PACK

A poster in the Braehead Shopping Centre urging people to buy shopping vouchers could have been better sited. It was stuck on a pillar in the gents' toilet and proclaimed: 'Splash out on a friend.'

A group of Faslane submariners were discussing the stress of leaving their families for long periods of time. We could not help overhearing the older, experienced chap who told the rest: 'You must be sensitive to your wives' emotional needs.' And after a pause he added: 'Never, ever, whistle while you pack.'

Funny how chaps become braver in the pub than they are at home. We don't think for a moment the loudmouth in the bar was telling the truth when he opined: 'I said to my wife, "You're getting old-looking. Have you seen the wrinkles you've got?" She told me they were not wrinkles, but laughter lines. So I told her, "Nothing could ever have been that funny."'

NEW TAIWAN
PORRIDGE
RESTAURANT

Harry Potter walks into a bar. The bartender says: 'We don't serve 12-year-olds.' Harry says: 'Hey, if I wanted the good stuff I wouldn't have come to this dive.'

☆ ☆ ☆

A letting agent was showing a young couple around a swanky New Town flat in Edinburgh, and having ascertained that they were interested in renting it, settled down to asking them a few formal questions. After quizzing them on their age, occupation and so on, she started quickly reeling off the rest of the list. 'Children?' 'Yes, two boys,' came the reply. This was duly noted by the letting agent, before she continued: 'Animals?' The female of the couple looked slightly offended and said: 'No, they're quite well behaved, actually.'

☆ ☆ ☆

Her voice was a little bit loud in the West End bar last night as she asked her friends: 'Do you know the only thing that divorce proves?' We confess to straining our ears for the words of wisdom to follow. 'Whose mother was right in the first place.'

☆ ☆ ☆

At the Thistle Hotel in Glasgow, where luminaries had gathered for a conference on innovation in Scotland, Sir Alan Langlands, the principal of Dundee University, was talking about how he had just returned to Scotland after having spent some time running the NHS in England. Sir Alan told delegates: 'Mrs Thatcher used to tell me she wanted the health service to be run like British

Airways and Marks & Spencer.' And judging by the state of those companies nowadays, he added: 'I think we've done a pretty fine job of it.'

We are told of a Radio Clyde talent contest at the King's Theatre. It seems that some of the losers were less than congratulatory towards those who had successfully made their way into the grand final. After one well-endowed girl had performed in a dangerously low-cut top, a disconsolate loser was heard to snipe: 'Aye, it was all right for her, she had Right Said Fred on stage with her.' For those puzzled by that remark it should be pointed out that RSF is a popular beat combo fronted by two bald-headed gentlemen.

A chap arrives home from his work to be quickly told by his harassed wife: 'We're invited to my sister's for dinner. You've got half-an-hour to change and argue about it.'

A surgeon from Glasgow tells us how he was visiting the Aston Martin factory in England, and was proudly shown how each car was hand-finished according to the tastes of the customer. His guide pointed out that there, writ large on the wall above each car, were the names of the individuals purchasing the vehicles. As they passed along the line of cars, the guide read out names like David Beckham and Eddie Irvine, until they came to the last one, at which point he said: 'Now, I don't think I need tell you who THIS one is for.' Reading the sign, the medic could only come up with: 'A prisoner of war?' He felt suitably embarrassed when he was informed that, no, the initials in fact stood for Prince of Wales.

☆ ☆ ☆

Plains in Lanarkshire is one of those villages that people cruelly describe as, 'the land that time forgot'. In Plains, someone of a republican mien, and there are a few there, has sprayed in giant letters on a wall: 'Remember the Easter Rising.' Someone, who we must congratulate for their sense of humour, has sprayed out 'Rising', and replaced it with 'Bunny'.

We are still trying to track down the company we were told about which promised its staff a new Toyota to the person who increased sales the most. An ecstatic salesperson heard she had won, and was then blindfolded and led to her prize. To her horror, when she whipped off the blindfold, she was confronted, not with a new car, but with a toy Yoda – you know, the little squashed-face guy from Star Wars. Oh, how they must have laughed in the management toilets.

Our stories about excuses for not attending committee meetings prompts mention of the player from Dalziel Rugby Club who could not attend meetings due to 'kidney trouble'. It seemed that he kidney be bothered, as he later confided.

A Glasgow mother tells us she was surprised and delighted when her teenage son brought the video of Jane Austen's *Sense and Sensibility* back from Blockbuster. At last he was finding a more sensitive side, she thought. Alas, no. After a few minutes watching, he gave up in disgust, explaining that he had assumed it was a follow-up to *Dumb and Dumber*.

Dundee music shop Groucho's in the Nethergate is celebrating its 25th year in business, and has compiled a list of the stranger requests from its fair share of *High Fidelity*-esque nutters. They include:

Upon asking a young lad if he has proof he is over 16, he replies: 'No, but I've got a fag packet.'

On viewing the James Bond *The Spy Who Loved Me* video, two

customers exclaim that the producers must have plagiarised the idea from Austin Powers. Or the following conversation. Customer: 'How much is the *Jesus of Nazareth*?' Salesperson: '£19.99.' Customer: 'How many videos is it?' Salesperson: 'Four.' Customer: 'Are they all about Jesus?'

The customer who wants records by Enigma, and goes to look under 'N'.

And, our favourite – Customer: 'Do you sell tickets for the Playhouse?' Assistant: 'Who for?' Customer: 'For myself . . . oh . . . I mean *Evita*.'

Shop assistants are really hitting back through *The Diary*. The latest works in a large tile emporium in Glasgow, where he was approached by a customer wanting to order some additional tiles to complete a kitchen renovation. The assistant asked what make they were. The customer was ready as she had looked at the box containing the others before going to the store. 'Muyfragil,' she told him.

We mentioned the odd requests of customers at Groucho's record store in Dundee. Ninian Fergus of Edinburgh, also from the music trade, recalls the following conversation with a customer. 'Have you got that CD by that band advertised last night on the telly?' 'What was the name of the band?' 'Aw, a dinnae ken.' 'Well, do you know what the CD is called?' 'Oh aye – their *Greatest Hits*.'

A little tale of thieving in Renfrewshire where a chap walked into a supermarket last week, perused the electronic equipment, and casually walked out with a nice new DVD player, without stopping at the check-out. A rerun of the security cameras shows the miscreant, but by then it is too late. But next day, who should turn up at the customer service desk to complain that his new DVD player he had 'bought' the day before did not have a remote control? Yes, said thief who was then nabbed by security.

Ayrshire. They do think differently there you know. A reader from Irvine stopped at a café in Mauchline and read the menu board where, under 'Soup of the Day', the waitress had written: 'Same as yesterday.' And as our reader tells us: 'The funny thing was, no one in the café thought there was anything strange about that.'

☆ ☆ ☆

Forget your expensive trips to Lourdes if you are looking for a miracle – we would suggest St Dominic's in Bishopbriggs instead. We make such an outrageous claim because of a paragraph in the church's newsletter which tells us: 'Following on from the finding of a set of crutches in the chapel grounds last week, a wheelchair, two zimmer frames, and a disregarded plaster cast have been found in the vicinity of the church.'

☆ ☆ ☆

We're not sure if this is a true story or not, but just very occasionally we let them in after checking as much as we can. It concerns a chap at an agricultural show who spots a 'name-the-sheep' competition, and asks his young daughter to have a go. She decides she likes the name 'Fluffy Cloud', and her adoring father dutifully writes it down on an entry slip and places it in the box. Later on, he hears the announcer saying: 'We had a lot of fine entries for the 'name-the-sheep' competition, the best of which was "Fluffy Cloud".' That prompted a squeal of delight from the daughter, until the announcer continued: 'Unfortunately, the correct answer was a 'North Ronaldsay'.

Radio Scotland no longer carries the lunchtime fishmarket report. Unfortunately, the company that sends out the programme details to newspapers, which are known as billings, is still erroneously including the fishmarket report. An inquiry is being launched into how this could happen. It is known internally as, inevitably, Billingsgate.

Those of a nervous disposition skip this one. It is a warning to be careful what you do in the bedroom. A Glasgow woman enters said room and espies one of those cardboard tubes of Pringles crisps. Giving it a shake she realises there are only a few crumbs left, but being peckish she takes off the lid and pours them into her mouth. It is that precise moment she discovers exactly what her husband does with his toe-nail clippings after going at them with the scissors in the bedroom.

☆ ☆ ☆

At Pitlochry Highland Games the other week, the frightfully posh announcer is commentating on the event where you hurl a heavy weight over a bar. Trying to inject some colourful urgency into what can be a fairly pedestrian experience, he tells the crowd: 'That attempt was the equivalent of throwing a seven-year-old child over a double-decker bus.' 'Now that would really spice up the games,' murmured one non-child-owning spectator.

Sports presenter Tam Cowan, reminiscing about Airdrie, tells us: 'The last time I was in Airdrie this local guy said to me, "Do you want to share a taxi?" I said, "Fair enough." So he said, "Right, I'll have the engine, and you can take the wheels".'

MUNICIPAL MATTERS

This tale is from a Glasgow councillor, so it may well be true. A busload of tourists of many nationalities is about to set off on the city bus tour. The guide says: 'Before we depart, on your right you can see George Square with its many statues of the great figures in history who have contributed so much to this fine city.' A Glaswegian, much the worse for drink and unable to mind his own business, makes a loud contribution from the pavement. It is a short expression of his opinions which, if we were to repeat it here, would be replete with asterisks. Ignoring the alternative city guide, the lady on the bus continued: 'Standing on the east side of the square you can see the magnificent Glasgow City Chambers, opened in 1888, where the bailies and councillors of the city deliberate on the great issues of the day on behalf of its citizens.' This was met by a further contribution of asterisks from our inebriated friend. As the bus moved off, the guide announced: 'And, if you look to your left, the gentleman who is about to bid us farewell is the Lord Provost of Edinburgh.'

Glasgow's municipal minds were discussing wedlock at the City Chambers yesterday. New rules mean civil marriages can now take place anywhere outside a registry office, providing it has sufficient 'solemnity and dignity'. The SNP's John Mason thought that was too restrictive. 'If someone wants to get married on the Glasgow Underground at midnight, then why shouldn't they be able to?' he demanded. 'Because it shuts at 11,' sighed Charlie Gordon, the council leader.

The Northern Ireland peace process appeared to have reached its zenith last week when Glasgow City Council received a grant application from the IRA to stage a street party for the Queen's Jubilee. Closer inspection revealed the application had in fact come from the Inchmurrin Residents Association on the south side of the city.

Aberdeen Council, it seems, is about to take a very tough line on the problem of run-down schools. At a recent Labour Party meeting, the discussion had just moved on from Afghanistan, and in particular the costs of the weapons used in waging war on the Taliban, to the closer-to-home problems of school repairs. One councillor told the meeting that a school in his ward needed half-a-million pounds worth of repairs. 'That might sound like a lot,' he said, 'but one cruise missile would solve the problems overnight.'

Glasgow's council officers who accompany the provost and bailies on civic duties have to wear green frock coats and high starched collars as their uniform. After a particularly lengthy function, one of the officers was glad to discard the tight collar which had been biting into his neck, and head for his local boozer. It was there that a good samaritan, seeing the red line around his neck, tried to cheer him up by saying that no matter what gets you down at this time of year, trying to take your own life was not the answer.

A reader from Cumbernauld, the town which had just been awarded the Plook on the Plinth accolade for being the most dismal architectural carbuncle in Scotland, asks: 'Airdrie last year, Cumbernauld this year. If

5th August 1953.

Owing to my previous nights illness I spent the morning in bed and the early part of the afternoon reading. At 5·30 I went to see Dr. Gavin Young about my nose; he discovered some blood vessels on the inside of the nose that caused the bleeding. He cauterised or burned them but thanks to the cocaine there was no pain. Went to bed at about 8 and read till 10·30.

another town in the area wins next year, does North Lanarkshire Council get to keep the trophy?'

Glasgow councillors decided on a site visit to a health and sauna club applying for a licence, just to make sure the premises were legitimately what they claimed to be. Back at the licensing board meeting a councillor, who had been intrigued by a large pole in the middle of the floor of the proposed sauna, feared it might have had some connection with pole dancing, where comely young women writhe for the titillation of leering male clients. 'What's the pole for?' he barked at the woman applying for the licence. 'Callisthenics,' she replied without a moment's hesitation.

The scene is a recent civic function in Glasgow. A lady councillor arrives slightly flushed and apologising for being late due to work commitments. She explains to Lord Provost Alex Mosson: 'Sorry, I'm just off a plane.' The Lord Provost, affecting to misunderstand, replies: 'Och, don't worry. Just put on a wee bit of lippy and you'll look fine.'

The trials and tribulations of being a councillor. Dumbarton councillor Linda McColl was visiting an old folks' home in her ward when she came across an old fellow who seemed to be in some distress clinging to a railing outside the door. Going over to help, she asked him what was wrong. 'I've soiled myself,' he told her, in a perhaps plainer way than we have recorded it. 'I'll go and get a member of staff,' Linda told him. After quickly thinking this over, he replied: 'Wait five minutes, hen. I've no finished.'

☆ ☆ ☆

Councillor Ann Watters in Fife has been expressing her concern that the normal process of painting the Forth Bridge has apparently been disrupted. Which gave the local newspaper, the *Fife Free Press*, the opportunity to run a class headline: 'Watters troubled over bridge'.

☆ ☆ ☆

Council schemes to encourage kids to eat more fruit and veg still have an uphill struggle it seems. Reader David Mungall of Glasgow's south side was in his local Asda in Toryglen when the check-out girl came across an item she failed to recognise. In order to price it, she asked him what it was. 'Broccoli,' he had to explain.

☆ ☆ ☆

You expect some respect to be offered to a city's Lord Provost – but obviously not by Australians. Alex Mosson, Glasgow's LP, was receiving a delegation of visiting young Aussies. One of them asked if he could have a personal word with the Lord Provost. This young fellow, of Scots descent and very well cognisant of the footballing divides in Glasgow, shook Mr Mosson by the hand and said: 'This is the hand that shook the hand of Dick Advocaat at Ibrox this week.' The LP smiled diplomatically and said: 'And this is the hand that shook the hand of his holiness, the Pope, in Rome two weeks ago.'

We are often told tales of the white settlers in the North of Scotland who do not always blend well with the indigenous population. A northern reader claims that a new neighbour rang Highland Council to request the removal of the Deer Crossing sign on the road. The reason given was that too many deer were being hit by cars and he no longer wanted them to cross there.

Councillors in Renfrewshire were delighted to hear that Paisley Art Gallery had been gifted a number of paintings as part of the Saatchi Bequest, which involves distributing contemporary art to the regions. The council report listed the paintings as 'Swimsuit', 'Corset', 'Chair', 'Not Without an Element of Frustration', 'Mr Reasonable', and 'Delightful'. A puzzled councillor reading the list just had to ask: 'Are these paintings, or the start of a Mills & Boon novel?'

The scene is a Kilsyth funeral parlour. The family of the dearly departed thought they had finally negotiated the expensive financial aspects of the burial arrangements when a further bombshell was dropped upon them. Although the dear departed old lady in question had been born and bred in Kilsyth, she had later in life moved away from the district in order to be nearer her daughter. In the eyes of the local council, this made her an outsider and as such liable to a £600 surcharge for having the family lair reopened. This act of grave-robbery caused the son-in-law, who had up until then kept stoically quiet over the serious dent being made in his bank balance, to leap to his feet and shout: 'Who's opening the bloody lair then? Elaine C. Smith?'

POLITICS

When not up to his oxters in Balkan conflict and other geopolitical crises, Lord Robertson of Nato likes to get back to Scotland for a spot of R&R. But wherever George goes, whether it be a Hamilton Accies football match or for a pint in his local, he is accompanied by two Nato minders. Lord Robertson likes to be as informal as possible, going about as an ordinary citizen. Which is why he recently had to phone his car insurers to add the names of his two minders to his motor policy. 'Who are these people?' asked the girl at the other end of the line. 'Personal security personnel,' he replied. The girl asked for some clarification. 'Bodyguards,' explained Lord Robertson. 'Why do you need bodyguards?' the girl asked in an amiably nosy Scottish call-centre worker way. 'I'm Secretary-General of Nato,' George told her. 'Hang on,' said the girl, checking her computer. 'We've got your job down here as a secretary,' she said. 'Just leave it as that', said Lord Robertson, 'the premium will be cheaper'.

As criticism continues over the conditions at Barlinnie Prison, we are reminded of a slight culture clash when SNP MSP Christine Grahame visited the jail on one of those fact-finding missions politicians enjoy. Christine is chatting to one of the inmates, who tells her he has two nine-year-old daughters. 'Ah, twins,' says Christine, thinking what a happy event their births must have been. 'Naw,' replies the prisoner, puncturing her reverie. 'Two different wimmin.'

SNP MSP Linda Fabiani was given a written briefing from the British Embassy in Germany to acquaint her with the background on Saxony, as she was meeting representatives from the Saxony Laender at the Scottish Parliament. She was wondering how the briefing would cover the history of Dresden, its largest town. And in best *Yes, Minister* fashion, the briefing document states: 'Probably Britain's locally best-known link with Dresden has been its contribution to the rebuilding of the Frauenkirche, the most famous of the churches destroyed by Allied bombing in 1945.' Sounds a bit like the 'a big boy did it and ran away' rewriting of history.

☆ ☆ ☆

New finance minister Andy Kerr was visiting the begging bowl councillors at COSLA, where the president, Pat Watters, reminded Andy that the last time they had met, Pat was a Strathclyde regional councillor in the '80s, and Andy was a student militant who showered councillors with flour from the public benches in some protest over student loans. Unfazed at being outed as a protester – not very New Labour after all – Andy eyed Pat's now greying locks and commented: 'And I see you've still not managed to get all the flour out.'

☆ ☆ ☆

Our MSPs through in Edinburgh opened their mail to discover they had all been sent Valentine cards from the Impotence Association. It was not meant personally, they were pleased to discover, only an attempt by the association to highlight the need to offer more treatment on the NHS for sufferers. Sadly, one red-faced politician did not read the card properly, and was bragging to everyone that he had been singled out for a card from the Importance Association – until someone deflated his ego.

☆ ☆ ☆

Enterprise Minister Iain Gray, taking over from Wendy Alexander,

spoke at Caledonian University urging children from deprived areas to go to uni. The new minister said that some children didn't want to attend university because they thought it was only for 'squares' and 'posh' kids. Which prompted one boy from St Joseph's Primary in Blantyre, to blurt out: 'I know that. My auntie went to uni – and she wisnae posh.'

Leave Wendy Alexander alone, for goodness sake. She's a lovely woman. And we rightly condemn the civil servant at the Scottish Executive who claims that a colleague who worked for her when she was Minister for Everything was getting fed up with her devotion to detail and telephoning at all hours of the day and night. As he said to a colleague: 'Can you think of anything worse than been woken up by a phone call from Wendy at 2.30 in the morning?' 'Yes,' his colleague replied. 'A nudge.'

Bitte notieren Sie
notwendige Reparaturen
auf der Rückseite

•••

Would you be so kind as
to let us know of any
necessary repairs
on the backside

Scotland's deputy health minister, Hugh Henry, was a little unsteady on his feet at the launch of Argyll and Clyde Health Board's strategy for older people. He burst an eardrum at the weekend, which affected his balance. Or, as Hugh told his audience: 'It's a Paisley man's dream – getting that magic swaying feeling without having to buy five pints first.'

☆ ☆ ☆

It is a tough enough job being a parliamentarian in North Lanarkshire without comedians putting in their tuppence worth.

The occasion was the recent Red Rose dinner, the annual bash held by the Motherwell and Wishaw Labour constituency party. Frank Roy and Jack McConnell, respectively the MP and MSP for the twin cities of the plain, were in attendance and were joined at the top table by Dr John Reid, fellow Lanarkshire Labour MP. The turn for the evening was John McKelvie, former senior polisman turned after-dinner speaker. Picking off each politico in turn, Mr McKelvie said who would have believed that we would have a man on the moon and Jack McConnell would be first minister. 'Pity we got it the wrong way round,' he added. Mr McKelvie revealed that when Frank Roy worked at the Ravenscraig steelworks, he was suspected of stealing equipment from the stores. 'I was on the case and went up to his mother's house. I asked her if she minded me taking a walk up the back of the garden and having a look in the shed. She replied, "Don't bother walking, son, just jump on the conveyor belt".'

☆ ☆ ☆

Some elderly chaps, calling

themselves the Antonine Guard, dressed up as Roman centurions, foot-soldiers, and so on, to march on the Scottish Parliament to complain about damage being done to old Roman roads. Although there were only five of them who turned up in full rig-out, Lothian and Borders Police were nevertheless out in reasonable numbers to help the marchers through the traffic lights. A woman could not stop her curiosity and went up to the polis in the High Street and asked why they were there. So the officer told her: 'We're waiting for a Roman invasion,' which is pretty good for a cop. At that the woman looked surprised and blurted out: 'What? Catholics?' Which says a lot about Scotland really.

The story going around the SNP is that security was so tight at Labour's Brighton conference that delegates had to answer questions about the Labour Party just to check they were bona fide delegates. So when one New Labour bright thing was asked who Keir Hardie was, he confidently answered, 'Stan Laurel's sidekick,' before striding on into the hall. Non-delegates were caught out, it is said, by being able to spell 'socialism'.

At a Tory party conference at Blackpool, the BBC's Westminster reporter, Jamie McIvor, was dining with David McLetchie, leader of the Scottish Parliament Tories. When the waiter asked if they would like coffees after the meal, Jamie piped up that yes, he would like a cappuccino. The waiter merely leaned forward and told him: 'I'm sorry sir, you're a little too far north for that sort of thing.'

☆ ☆ ☆

Ayrshire MP Brian Donohoe spent a number of weeks shadowing police officers to gain insight into their duties. A final assignment was at Ibrox for the Rangers–Dynamo Moscow game. An approaching female fan was carrying a shawl, and an officer had a look, expecting to have a discussion about the advisability of taking a baby to the match. But on peering inside he discovered a rabbit. She was questioned closely on whether she had intentions of releasing it on the pitch in some bizarre protest, but she actually told the officers that it was only her pet rabbit which had been to matches before, and seemed to enjoy it. No doubt she thought that four lucky rabbit's feet were better than one. But she still didn't get in. What gave him more food for thought was the Moscow manager going on to the Rangers bus after the match. When Brian asked the police what the problem was, he was told the manager was asking for the Moscow strips back, which had been swopped after the game, as the club didn't have any to spare.

Members of the Scottish Parliament's justice committee were touring Glasgow's Barlinnie Prison to see for themselves the crowded conditions, and how the staff tackle the prison's drug problem. One MSP asks a prisoner who has completed a drug treatment course where he was from. 'Castlemilk,' he replied. 'And where did you start taking drugs?' continued the MSP. 'Polmont,' said the prisoner. As the MSP's knowledge of Polmont was seeing the station while en route from Glasgow to Edinburgh, the puzzled politician added: 'That seems awfully far to go from Castlemilk to get drugs.' And the patient prisoner replied: 'I was in the Young Offenders' Institute there.'

Our thoughts on whether there are any Scottish parallels with the US presidential voting fiasco in Florida takes us to the Cathcart constituency in Glasgow – and no, not simply because Mount Florida railway station is in it. Tom Harris, the prospective Labour candidate, recalls an election count when the candidates were gathered around the returning officer discussing the spoiled papers and whether they should be allowed. In dispute was one ballot paper on which in the box opposite the name of the then Labour candidate, John Maxton,

Sir Sean put off swing by children

SCREEN LEGEND Sir Sean Connery told the annual meeting of his exclusive golf club he was fed up with badly

someone had written in tiny, neat letters: 'They're all lying bastards, but this one isn't as bad as the rest.' Maxton successfully argued that was clearly a vote for him, and it was indeed given to him by the returning officer. So much more fun than a simple cross, isn't it?

☆ ☆ ☆

That story reminded reader Archie Flockhart of the time a Jewish Labour MP was a candidate. One of the polling papers was scrawled with obscenities and a swastika was drawn next to his name. The returning officer coolly remarked: 'Well, it's an unusual shape of cross, but it is definitely a cross,' and awarded him the vote.

☆ ☆ ☆

How impressive is the ability of some of our politicians to think quickly. Step forward Scottish Secretary and Minister for Explaining Government Disasters John Reid. Being interviewed by the BBC at Brighton, his words are being drowned out by a humming noise in the background. 'Sounds like a woman Hoovering,' he jauntily declares. A BBC politically-correct type replies: 'Why do you assume it's a woman?' John replies: 'It sounds much quicker than a man would do it.'

☆ ☆ ☆

The scene is the entrance to the TUC conference at the SECC and the inevitable demonstrations outside. A group of Iraqis have a drum which they keep pounding. Other demonstrators in support of the Palestinians have a quick confab then send over a spokesman who gives the Iraqis the classic line: 'Please can you be quiet? No one can hear us shouting.'

Colourful rebel Labour MP Tommy Graham is shopping in Costco, the discount supermarket, and is strolling past a books display when he is hailed by a Renfrewshire constituent. Tommy chats to the chap, who is with his young son. The child has picked up the latest Harry Potter book to buy. His school class has been studying politics, so the excited little lad pipes up: 'I know who you are. You're our MP.' So chuffed is he to meet Tommy that he asks the MP to sign the only thing he has available – his Harry Potter book. Just as Tommy starts to sign it, another customer who has picked up a Harry Potter tome sees the impromptu signing session and says: 'Will you sign mine as well?' 'Why?' asks Tommy, fearing a wind-up. 'Didn't you write it?' says the puzzled shopper who was applying the age-old maxim of if you see a queue, join it. But summoning up all his literary knowledge, Tommy was able to tell him: 'Don't be daft. A burd wrote it.'

Alex Salmond, former leader of the SNP, was one of many politicians grilled about whether they had ever smoked cannabis. Eck's reply was remarkably forthright: 'If you say "yes" people claim you're encouraging and supporting it, and if you say "no" it looks like you're a prick.' It appeared that Mr Salmond was taking a devil-may-care attitude now he is no longer in a political straitjacket. Or he may have thought the P-word was appropriate for a newspaper such as *The Guardian*. The truth, alas, is neither. The next day *The Guardian* gave the apology: 'Mr Salmond asks us to make it clear that what he actually said was "prig" not "prick".'

SPORTING TYPES

Lenzie Rugby Club had its finest moment recently when it won the SRU Bowl at Murrayfield. Coach Iain MacCallum met a rather posh SRU official at Murrayfield who had forgotten to introduce himself, so eventually Iain said to him: 'Who are you?' The Edinburgh chap replied: 'Fine, thank you. How are you?'

At the inaugural Rugby League World Cup game at Firhill, the Scottish team playing the Maoris had no Scots-born players, but was composed entirely of Australians and Englishmen. As they trooped off after losing by one point in a close-fought game, a group of teenagers chanted at them: 'How does it feel to be a Scot?'

Golfers at Old Prestwick Club have been very impressed with the palatial and expensive upgrading of the gentlemen's toilets and changing-rooms, carried out in time for a prestigious amateur tournament. One enthusiastic golfer, telling his wife about the changes, announced: 'Would you believe it, they have little tables with copies of *Country Life* and *Scottish Field* in the toilets.' His puzzled better half told him: 'After all the money you tell me they have spent, you would have thought they could afford toilet paper.'

A chap having a pint and watching on the pub telly that David Coulthard had won the Monaco Grand Prix, turned to his mate and said: 'Fantastic win, isn't it?' But, after thinking about it for a moment, his pal replied grudgingly: 'I suppose so. But Coulthard stays in Monaco. He'll know the roads.'

☆ ☆ ☆

With curling on the telly at the Winter Olympics we are told of a rink not quite up to Olympic standards where a game old chap of 85 had not the best of eyesight, so his skip held a flashlight on his broom handle to give him the line for the shot. A chap, watching from the next rink, was heard to mutter: 'If I was 85 and saw a bright light ahead of me, I'd turn and go the other way.'

☆ ☆ ☆

When the Edinburgh rugby team signed New Zealander Brendan Laney, the club's PR man, Malcolm

Brown, nipped into a tool hire shop in Gorgie Road to borrow a chainsaw for Brendan to pose with, as Chainsaw is his nickname back in NZ – yes, that is, indeed, how the PR mind works. While waiting inside he hears that two Blue Meanies are outside writing tickets, so Malcolm dashes out to remonstrate that he will only be a minute. Of course, his plea falls on deaf ears and his silver Celica is given the dreaded parking penalty. Disgruntled, he returns to the shop, collects his chainsaw, and on the way out bumps into the warden again who eyes him up and tells him: 'Christ Almighty, it's only a parking ticket.'

☆ ☆ ☆

Golfers are, generally, a douce breed, but they can still on occasion be a little unkind. Witness a foursome playing off the 16th tee on the Ferntower Course at Crieff Golf Club. A portly gentleman, having topped his drive along the fairway, was giving vent to his feelings when he was told by his friend: 'You're OK, you're OK, it's a Sally Gunnell shot.' Asked to elaborate, the chap continued: 'It's not very good looking, but it's a runner.'

Another odd golfing term? A reader tells us that he and his mates play an 'Adolf and Eva' rule: they only ever count two shots in the bunker.

To the Pulse gym at Leith Victoria Leisure Centre where two larger gentlemen are peching and panting on the running machines. One of the would-be sylphs slips and crashes to the ground. His friend leaps to his aid and asks if he is okay. Taking the proffered hand, the fallen Leviathan levers himself upright and mournfully checks the kilojoule counter on his running machine: '240 kilojoules, that's the sausages aff this morning's fry-up.' Showing true Olympian spirit, he then clambers back on to the machine and starts jogging away while announcing: 'Now for the bacon.'

PARONOMASIA

We're not too proud to plagiarise from a New York magazine's competition where readers were asked to take a well-known expression in a foreign language, change one letter, and create a whole new meaning:

- Respondez, s'il vous plaid: Honk if you're Scottish.
- Harlez-vous francais?: Can you drive a French motorcycle?
- Que sera, serf: Life is feudal.
- Pro bozo publico: Support your local clown.
- Haste cuisine: French fast-food.
- Quip pro quo: A fast retort.

Willie More, a Barrhead refugee who sought asylum in Birmingham, suggests:
- Tardyloo: I'll wait until the smell has gone.
- Tarte blanche: A meringue in any shape you want.
- C'est la vin: I forget.
- A la carse: A picnic near Stirling.

Christine Martin offers:
- Comment allez-yous?: A traditional west of Scotland greeting.

stevon1968 (all our readers used to have names but some are now known only by e-mail addresses) comes up with:

- Bona fido: Good dog.
- Ipso fatso: Who ate all the pies?
- In fragrante delicto: Mary Archer?

We should also slip in Gordon Armstrong's Jeus ex machina: ginger from the vending machine.

And Ludovic Thierry's Pox romana: remembering to pack your condoms when visiting Italy; and Crape Suzette: Suzette learned to cook in Scotland.

Alan Alexander, who gives his address as Dull, Aberfeldy – at least we think it's his address – offers:

- Grands vans de Bordeaux: Lorry-loads of red biddy.
- Casus belti: Why teachers used to hit weans.
- Altar ego: Self-regarding cleric.
- Par diem: Day return to Dunfermline.
- Per anum: Best place for all of the above.

Norman Ferguson of Edinburgh takes a Germanic tack with:

- Was ist daz? Is this washing powder?
- Was ist klos? What is wrong with Rangers' goalie?
- Guten taf: A Welshman admired in Germany.

Christina Andrew-Wellman suggests: Persona non gratin: I'm cheesed off with him.

Alan Alexander of Aberfeldy puts forward: Le mat juste: nae linoleum.

Annie Thorne offers: Dipso facto: he's definitely drunk.

Jim Nicol of Lenzie sends Raisin d'etre: The need for dried fruit; Farce majeure: A daft carry-on; and Beau teste: Nice ball.

Johnny Miller, without doubt the cleverest Glaswegian working as a librarian on the *San Francisco Chronicle*, picks up the theme with Dis Kapital: Make jokes about Embra. A la carty: brought to your table on a trolley. Quo vodis: who drank the cairry-oot? Cine qua non: A must-see movie. A wee dick and Doris . . . maybe not.

PARONOMASIA

Bryce Scobie shows his erudition by heading his entry 'Paronomasia' which, as we didn't know, means a play on words which sound alike. Mr Scobie's erudition was, thankfully, balanced by the general bad taste of his suggestions. Dieu et mon droot: God, I could kill a pint. Pox vobiscum: I hope you get the clap. De fucto: You're screwed. Dropt de seigneur: I wouldn't touch her with a bargepole. Per arsua ad astra: Your bum's out the windae.

Then there was the variation of altering one letter in a film title. The city council takes on *Big Issue* sellers in a battle for possession of Buchanan Street: *A Farewell to Alms* (L. McGregor, Newton Mearns). The story of a shy woodland creature who grows up to manage Partick Thistle: *Lambi* (Paul Gardner).

A tale of three women throwing away their inhibitions on a Roman holiday: *Three Coils in a Fountain* (Jim Drysdale of Hamilton).

A vampire spoof set in Glasgow: *Don't Sook Now* (Ken McMaster of Clydebank).

A tale of Old Firm bias in Glasgow's city chambers: *How Green Was My Lalley* (David Wood of Arden, Glasgow).

A Scotsman finding a job as a painter and decorator in a Western town: *Hang 'em Hugh* (Murdo Macdonald of Bridge of Weir).

A good-time Glasgow girl who drinks only pink wine: *The Slapper and the Rose* (Peter Mackay of Greenock).

To Save and Have Not: harrowing tales of Equitable Life investors (Ken Johnson, Lochwinnoch).

Gregory's Giro: a gangly Scottish actor finds work harder and harder to come by (Calum Morrison).

There's a Girl in My Coup: romantic comedy set in a land-fill site.

Where the Buffalo Foam: foot-and-mouth hits the US prairies.

The Cruel Tea: only one scone left in Morningside.

Shand: a lone accordionist faces down the bad guys. *Showgoat*: Paul Robeson sings at the Milnathort Agricultural Show.

My Sair Lady: another late Friday night.

Buffy the Vampire Slater: beware the wee flat blood-suckers (all the above from Ken McKenzie, Clarkston).

The Tiree Amigos: a group of friends have a rollicking night out in Ballavoulin.

Raging Mull: a Calmac ferry strike disrupts whisky supplies.

Muck Rogers in the 25th Century: futuristic sex comedy set in an island community (all three Hebridean movies from Larry Gervais).

Rogue Grader: the SQA story. *Greash!*: Sir Sean in a 1950s' high school romp.

M*E*S*H: Bearsden doctor is seconded to US field hospital (all from David Wood, Arden, Glasgow).

Vertical Simit: Rab C. Nesbit goes rock-climbing (Gillian Madden.) *Taxi Drivel*: philosophical ramblings from the paralytically drunk inhabitants of a late-night Dundee taxi queue (Laurence Hayden, Essex).

Once Upon A Time In The Vest: Rab C. Nesbitt rides (Ian Johnstone, Bournemouth). *How the Vest Was Won*: Rab C. Nesbitt rides again (Kenny Murray, Ayr).

Bun Fight at the OK Corral: Stanley Baker and Robert Donat in shoot-out to decide who will end up in the fly cemetery (Gordon Forbes, Port Glasgow).

Sodden Impact: documentary on the conditions at Scottish football terraces in the days before the Criminal Justice Act (Jim McCrudden).

High Noun: blow-by-blow account of the world Scrabble championships (Jim Robertson, Cambuslang).

True Crit: biopic about John Wayne, with honest assessment of acting ability (Gerry MacKenzie, Bearsden).

Ryan's Laughter: contemporary Celtic Tiger film following a Dublin man going to his bank (Gerry Boyce).

The Thin Red Link: a Scots butcher is accused of selling inferior sausages (Julie Marshall, Prestwick).

Loonraker: Aberdonian spy searches for vital information in enemy wheelie-bins (Archie Russell, Motherwell).

Dead Ports Society: documentary on the demise of Port Glasgow Co-op. *The Blue Limp*: sporting biopic of any new Rangers signing. *Snot White and the Leven Dwarfs*: Fife girl leads teenie gang (all from Alex McCrossan, Glasgow).

The Road to Dali: Bob Hope and Bing Crosby discover surrealism. *Stir Wars*: Ken Hom and Delia Smith cross woks. *Gone with the Wand*: Scarlett O'Hara elopes with Harry Potter (all three from Willie Smith, Dunblane). *Who Flamed Roger Rabbit?*: murder mystery set in Burger King. *Love Me Fender*: story of a musician infatuated by his guitar. *Lear Window*: housebound James Stewart watches neighbours performing Shakespeare (Angus Macmillan, Dumfries).

Highlender: an everyday tale of loan sharking in Niddrie (Gail Fairman, Athens). *Where Eagles Date*: wildlife romance set in Balquhidder (Linda Ormiston). *Toga! Toga! Toga!*: a sequel to Gladiator. *Bin Her*: dyslexic man decides to seek a divorce (Ronnie Johnston, Newlands).

The Pyjama Gape: Rock Hudson reveals more than he intended to Doris Day (Julie Marshall, Prestwick).

Hooray for Holyrood: a joyous musical about architects, surveyors, and other construction professionals delighted with the flexibility of the budget for the new Scottish Parliament building (John H. McColl, Chicago).

Rust for Life: story of the Lada motor car (G. Lambie, Larkhall).

Flute: Donald Sutherland and Jane Fonda in detective yarn set in Larkhall (multiple contributions).

Bagsy: a group of Glasgow children stranded far from home with few resources discover who is the strongest and most assertive of their number (Murdo Macdonald).

*uck Soup: Groucho Marx dining in Rogano expresses wish to omit starter and proceed immediately to main course (Peter Stewart, Hamilton). *For Four Eyes Only*: James Bond movie for the optically challenged (Graeme MacKenzie, Isleornsay, Skye). *Guess Who's Coming to Pinner?*: Wimbledon FC's search for a new home down in the London stockbroker belt (Rab Jenkins, East Kilbride).

The Vital Shark: terrifying account of a series of attacks on West Coast puffers by a great white (George McGarry, Airdrie).

Some Like It Oot: two musicians on the run from the Mob hide out in a nudist camp. *Nutting Hill*: the Hugh Grant–Julia Roberts love story, set in Bridgeton (Peter Mackay, Greenock).

Hitchcock's *The Birts*: a small town is overrun by a plague of management consultants (Ian Johnstone, Bournemouth). Hitchcock's *The Bards*: a small Welsh town is overrun by a plague of poets (from multiple contributors).

The Sword and the Scone: tea-shop wars on the south side of Glasgow (Robbin Nichol. Yes, with two Bs. Yes, we know it sounds more like a crime than a name.)

The 39 Sheps: *Blue Peter* cloning experiment goes wrong (Gavin Stark, Aberdeen).

The Man Who Shod Liberty Valance: John Wayne plays a kindly but compulsive blacksmith (David Crane, Melbourne).

Born Fred: the story of a transsexual called Freda (Alice Grandison, Dollar).

The Dong Goodbye: sequel to above as hero/heroine has the op (Tom Donnelly, Glasgow).

Graham Richmond suggests a film where Michael Palin buys a new pair of trousers everywhere he stops – *Around the World in 80 Daks*.

James Waugh of Cumbernauld just adds the plaintive comment 'what an ex told me' to his suggestion – *White Men Can't Hump*.

Also on a dating theme, Aileen Caskie suggests a comedy about Scots chaps who misplace their keys after a Saturday night out – *The Pistman Always Rings Twice*. Which leads to Ayrshire's Scott Williamson's thriller about what's considered a right good night in Kilwinning – *sex, pies and videotapes*. Then, after a night out, there is a documentary, says Jim McDonald of Carluke, on how a Scottish working man allocates the cash left after a few pints on the way home from work – *The Remains of the Pay*.

Paul Kerr suggests the whimsical tale of a local parkie who tries to keep his green place free from loitering youths, with a great score by Isaac Hayes: *Shift!*

Ian Barnett of Newton Mearns comes up with *Gregory's Gird*, the story of a shy schoolboy who couldn't get a girl and takes up a traditional pursuit instead.

Kenny Murray of Ayr suggests a violent study of the world of professional bingo players – *A Man Called House*.

Angus Macmillan of Dumfries goes on the documentary trail with *Die Lard*, an examination of West of Scotland dietary habits. Not very couthy, but we enjoyed it, is Mr Macmillan's musical *Natural Born Tillers* – an enchanting story of a group of girls just born to dance.

William McNish – he comes from Cumnock so we forgive the earthiness – suggests the story of a man with prostate problems who goes to the NHS and has to wait so long that he can no longer manage the toilet: *Pission: Impossible*. And we thank Morag Dean for *The Big Steep*, a piece of film noir set in a Greenock washhouse.

Blame Tom Bowden of Polmont for *The Slapper and the Dose* and *The Magnificent Semen*. No, we will not go into detail of the plot lines.

Paul Cortopassi of Bonnybridge gives us *The African Queer*, a true story of romance among riverboat sailors in the dark continent. Gurmeet Mattu adds to the gay oeuvre with *Oklahomo!* Quite a few readers suggested *Three Men in a Goat*.

Some entries which have the merit of being clean: *A Tan for all Seasons*, the life story of Tommy Sheridan, MSP (Leonard Franchi, Alexandria). *Who Kilted Roger Rabbit?*: Scotland gets into the animation business (George Allan). *Don't Book Now*: a cautionary tale about the British travel industry (Alex Carmichael).

Bryce Scobie suggests *Bwaveheart*: Elmer Fudd in a reprise of the Mel Gibson role. *Mutiny On The Bouncy*: kiddies in soft play area revolt against their parents. *The Man who would be Bing*: adaptation of Kipling's tale about a young man's ambition to be a crooner.

On the Waferfront: drama based on Glasgow's ice-cream wars (Danny McDonald, Paisley). *The Mild Bunch*: a group of reformed outlaws go around mending fences and solving land disputes (Kim McCauley).

There have been a number of altered movies inspired by Aberdeen and its hinterlands, including *Sheepless in Seattle*, *High Loon*, *Shakespeare in Cove*, *For Your Ewes Only*, and *Neep Throat*.

For sheer silliness, Barry McGuire of Ayr puts forward *Don't Dook Now*, a public service film about the inadvisability of swimming on certain Scottish beaches. We should perhaps mention the tale of the waitress exacting revenge on a customer who never tips – *I Spit On Your Gravy* (Drew Smith, Saltcoats). A modern tale of the carnage caused by PMT – *Lady and the Cramp* (Celia Stevenson). A tale of Glasgow ladies of the night out in Blythswood Square on a very cold night – *Sliding Hoors* (anon). And an ex-Scotland goalie struggles to make a living as a nightclub owner in *fin-de-siecle* Paris – you've got it, *Moulin Rough* (Rab Jenkins, East Kilbride).

The Conservative Party plot in the '80s to get rid of its leader – *Inter the Dragon* (Andy Lamb, Strathaven). The staff of an army field hospital in Korea resort to marching to keep their sanity amid the horror of war – *S*A*S*H* (Graeme Sharp). And Fred West's war epic – *Paving Private Ryan* (The Mast Lads).

Ken McMaster of Clydebank comes up with *Sutureworld*, a drama set in any casualty unit any weekend. Brian Reilly from Greece, the country not the movie, suggests *The Burds*, directed by Alfred Hitchcock, the story of Frank McAvennie's romantic rise and fall, and *It's a Wonderful Wife*, directed by Frank Capra, dedicated to devoted wives who stand by their men no matter what (script by Jeffrey Archer).

The Rev. Richard Cameron of Scotstoun breaks the rules by adding instead of replacing a letter. But we liked his *Where Beagles Dare*, an animal-rights production about a group of dogs who mount a daring escape by cable car from a pharmaceutical company's mountain laboratory.

Stuart Crawford of Haddington came up with the following triple bill: *Lulu*: soldiers of the South Wales Borderers are trapped in a kraal in southern Africa and are attacked by hordes of ferocious red-haired singers from Glasgow. *The Nuns of Navarone*: an intrepid band of commandos blow up a convent in southern Europe. *Naked Gus*: an X-rated film made by Lord MacDonald of Tradeston before he became famous. Gus only made it because he 'needed the work'.

Tom White of Kelvinside came in with: *Dirty Hairy*: adventures of a less than choosy lassie frae Govan. *A Fistful of Collars*: life in the Glesga polis. *How to Succeed in Business Without Actually Frying*: son of a Scots-Italian family leaves the chip shop for a successful low-fat career.

Mark Couperwhite of Haddington offers: *Get Shirty*, a tailor and his customer fall out. *A Fridge too Far*: a man's attempts to sneak another beer ends in tragedy when his wife catches him.

Johnny Miller, our man in San Francisco, offers the following scenarios: *Hootsie*: an edgy, high-energy dramatisation of the life and times of the Alexander Brothers, a cross-dressing Scottish folk duo whose impact on Scottish culture cannot be underestimated. *The Silence of the Limbs*: the cast of *Riverdance* is stalked by a mad knee-capper. *The Loneliness of the Long-Distance Punner*: a sentimental study of a man obsessed with getting his name in the *Herald* Diary.

Brian Kelly suggests *Crouching Tizer, Hidden Dralon*. This, as you might have guessed, is a film about the perils of soft drinks and soft furnishings in Chinese restaurants.

Gone with the Wine could be the story of a Coatbridge boy who meets a Kelvinside girl but their love match is ruined by disagreements over the relative merits of Buckfast and chardonnay. *Last Mango in Paris*: much the same as the original film but the pat of butter is replaced by a piece of exotic fruit. *The 39 Stops*: not the John Buchan thriller, but a road movie set on the number 66 bus from Clydebank to East Kilbride. *Three Days of the Condom*: a radical parish priest lifts the Catholic church's prohibition on contraceptives, but only for the September weekend.

Take that rather ordinary little movie *You've Got Mail*. It has now spawned *You've Got Hail*, the life of a Scottish weather forecaster (Tom Gardiner). *You've Got Dail*: how the Irish won independence (Ian Black, Glasgow). *You've Got Bail*, the Ross Harper story (Craig Spence); and *You've Got Fail*, a docu-drama about the SQA (Alex Carmichael).

Ronnie McMillan offers *The Biro-Man of Alcatraz*, the tale of a prisoner who took 20 years to dig his way out with a ball-point pen. Paul Kerr suggests *It's a Wonderful Lift*, a film biography of Mr Otis of Chicago, who built the first elevator.

Also inspired by the Jimmy Stewart classic, Danny McDonald of Paisley goes for *It's a Wonderful Fife*, a film extolling the glories of the Kingdom in a double bill with *The Magnificent Leven*.

John Harris hints that Sir William Wallace, the great hero, might have had moments of self-doubt with his suggestion of *Bravefeart*. David Walker of Kilmacolm thinks up: *Enter the Aragon*: Bruce Lee faces his greatest terror in a pub in Glasgow's Byres Road; *The King and E*: Yul Brynner learns all about rave culture; and *Fartasia*: the sorcerer's apprentice learns how to make wind.

WHO IS JUDY POLE?

A south-side Glasgow lady, known for her good works in raising money for charity, tells us she telephoned a well-known Scottish hotel to ask if they could put up a prize for a raffle for the Guide Dogs for the Blind charity. 'We're raising money for the blind dogs,' she tells the chap on the phone. There is a pause, and he tells her: 'God bless, but would it not be better just putting them down?'

Two pals meet for their usual evening pint or two in a Coatbridge club. Eddie says he's going on holiday the following week and won't be in for his pint and game of dominoes. Wishing him a good time, his pal, Tam, asks: 'Can ye bring me some fags back?' 'Nae problem,' says Eddie, who promises to bring his pal 1,000 ciggies. Two weeks later he's handing them over, and Tam says: 'That's great. How much do I owe you.' He's shocked when Eddie says £200. 'My God, where the hell did you buy fags at that price?' 'Blackpool,' says Eddie.

We hear the true story of the English structural engineer working for Glasgow firm Halcrow Waterman who was attempting to get a local squad to remove material from a site as he was under a bit of pressure from the client. After ranting lengthily at the foreman, he eventually demanded to know when the material would be moved. The bored foreman told him: 'Ah've no' got a scooby, pal,' to which the exasperated chap from south of the Border pleaded: 'Well, go get one. Hire a Scooby if you have to. Just get this stuff removed.'

A hotel in Renfrewshire cheekily put up a sign stating *See Judy Pole Dancing*. A Diary reader was touched by his wife's naïvety when they drove past the sign and his good lady remarked: 'What's so special about that?' followed shortly afterwards by: 'And who's Judy Pole anyway?'

☆ ☆ ☆

Life on the streets of Rothesay, as chronicled in the crime columns of the *Buteman* newspaper: 'A female was tracked down by CCTV cameras after a local publican reported the theft of a door curtain from his premises. When police found the female, who gave her name as Superwoman, she was wearing

the curtain as a cape. Police discretion was used in this instance and the curtain was restored to its rightful owner.'

We have reported some very tall tales about the polis on Mull. The following is extremely far-fetched and comes into the category of stories we wish had a shred of truth. The Hebridean cops are interrogating a suspect. They place a metal colander on his head and attach wires from it to the office photocopier. The suspect is asked various questions and, every so often, a police officer presses the button and the copier issues a sheet of paper with the words 'He's lying.' (This message having been carefully placed in the copier.) According to the legend, the suspect, faced with this incontrovertible evidence, confessed.

☆ ☆ ☆

When the *Herald* moved out of its premises in Albion Street, it brought a stream of reminiscences about the Press Bar next door. It used to be called the Express Bar when, naturally enough, the *Scottish Daily Express* was printed

This Red Vin de Pays is grown on the slops of the Herault, in the south of France. It is the perfect match with stew, grilled meats and matured cheeses. To be served at 14/16°C.

there. Not that we are saying the McEntee family, who own it, are careful with their money, but when the *Express* moved, they simply got out the stepladders, unscrewed the E and the X on the sign, and hey presto, the Press Bar was created. A certain Magnus Magnusson was a young whizzkid on the *Express* in his 20s, and despite his present elder-statesman-of-television role, young Magnus got so heated in an argument with a colleague from the *Express* in the bar, that they had what in common parlance is known as a square go. Des McEntee ordered them out, and they ended the fisticuffs across the road in the then Greyfriars Kirk courtyard. We like to think that Des actually shouted at Magnus: 'You might have started it here, but you'll finish it across the road.'

Two Glasgow couples are telling their friends about their skiing trip to the rather upmarket Aspen, Colorado. It seems that one of the couples, Kieran and Cheryl, were at the top of the run when Kieran had one of his sudden nosebleeds, to which he is prone. He asks Cheryl to rummage around in the bag strapped to her waist for a tissue or anything to help staunch the flow. Down at the bottom of the run, friend Paul is chatting to some upmarket Americans and believes he is making a good impression. This is the life, he is thinking. Far better than the hurly-burly of Partick, he muses. He tells his new American pals that he is just waiting for his friend to ski down, which Kieran duly does – and arrives to say hello to the Americans with a tampon sticking out of each nostril.

☆ ☆ ☆

We are told of the Eaglesham businessman and his wife who thought it was time their children were old enough not to creep in and sleep with their mother while he was away on business. So, after telling them that they were now very grown-up and had to spend the entire night in their own beds, he went away on his latest trip. On return to a very busy Glasgow Airport he was met by his wife and children, at which point his son ran up and shouted in front of everyone: 'Good news Daddy. Nobody slept with Mummy while you were away.'

☆ ☆ ☆

The technology at such keep-fit places as the David Lloyd centres becomes more and more advanced. An exercise bike with a 'fat burn' mode requires the user to enter various personal details including age. A lady of the Diary's acquaintance insists, of course, on lopping a good 20 years off her keyed-in answer. Which makes the regime that more difficult and puts years on her.

☆ ☆ ☆

We are told the true story of Lachie, on one of the islands, who goes to his local boozer where his usual drinking companions are looking quite animated. He pulls out a large bottle of whisky with an old label, which is half full, and tells them: 'It's my 80th birthday today and my father presented this bottle of Talisker to me on my 21st birthday after buying it on the day I was born. I only have a nip on special birthdays and I would like you to join me on my 80th.' After giving his pals a half he is putting the bottle back in his pocket when a chum who had drained his glass tells him: 'Lachie. How long d'you think you're going to live? Get that bottle back out.'

☆ ☆ ☆

It is a trying time when funeral arrangements have to be made for a departed loved one. Especially when a suitable time and place is not available for that last goodbye. A Glasgow woman whose husband had died was anxious that the cremation service be held at Linn Crematorium. Unfortunately, due to demand and a bank holiday, the only date on offer was a full week ahead. Disappointed but still hopeful, the lady said: 'It looks as if we might have to go elsewhere but could you let me know if you get a cancellation.'

A medical practitioner tells us of the simple ready-reckoner which he uses to adjust answers from male patients to certain questions. Number of cigarettes smoked: multiply by two. Units of alcohol consumed: multiply by three. Frequency of sexual intercourse: divide by four.

Gillian Lumsden of Motherwell was attending her doctor's surgery and, after taking her seat in the waiting-room and picking up the obligatory year-old magazine, found herself drawn to the conversation among three old biddies who were obvious regulars. Says Gillian: 'My ears pricked up when one confided to the other: "My tits aren't what they used to be." Well, myself and the wee embarrassed man behind me held our breath with anticipation. We were helpfully provided with the diagnosis from her friend who said: "That'll be because your neighbours have got that new cat."'

We hear of a woman in Milngavie who answered her phone at one in the morning to hear a young woman tell her without preamble: 'It's Susan here, Mum. I know I promised faithfully that Ian would have me home by midnight, but he really did have a puncture in his dad's car, and we've only just got it changed and made it to a phone box. Please don't be too angry.' Realising the girl had phoned the wrong number, the woman tried to be helpful by telling her: 'I'm sorry. I don't have a daughter named Susan.' There was a pause, and the girl told her: 'Look Mum, I knew you'd be upset, but you don't have to go overboard.'

Tina Turner was at Hampden, which brought a horde of fans to the Clockwork Beer Company bar in Cathcart. One wee wumman, of years almost as advanced as Tina, asked a member of staff: 'Whit's your special?' The chap glanced at the blackboard and began to recite: 'Our special today is breaded lobster tails on a selection of salad leaves with a marie-rose dip. It is served with carrots julienne and baby sweetcorn and a choice of potatoes, croquettes, hash browns, or French fries.' At that, the woman put on a pained expression and told him: 'Naw, your special. Is it Tennent's?'

The former Scottish miners' leader, Mick McGahey, was being fondly remembered by an official at the Chinese Embassy, who recently met some Scottish trade unionists. The official told them: 'We were with Mr McGahey at a reception where he taught us the Scottish custom of one for the road. Then there was another for the road, and then many for the road. Eventually I had to say to him: "Even Chairman Mao never walked a road as long as this."'

The chief executive of the Weir Group, Sir Ron Garrick, was guest of honour at Springburn College's prize-giving in Glasgow City Chambers. The chairman of the college board is giving a lengthy introduction to Sir Ron which involves reading out every cough and wind noise from his CV, detailing every job and directorship he has held since leaving school. After what seems like an eternity of this, one of the guests is heard saying to the person next to him: 'This chap Garrick doesn't seem to be able to hold down a job for long, does he?'

A young Edinburgh mother, having lunch with a pal in a smart

請勿在渡輪上募捐或傳道
NO DONATION & SERMON

George Street restaurant, was explaining how harassed she was, getting all the housework done. Her friend, draining a large chardonnay, told her: 'My idea of housework is to sweep the room with a glance.'

We are told of the Glasgow businessman who, arriving back at the airport from a trip abroad, decides rather reluctantly to buy his wife a belated present. Looking at perfumes, he discounts the £50 bottle, then the £25 eau de cologne, before telling the young assistant: 'Can you not show me something really cheap?' Without a word she hands him a mirror from the counter.

BLOODY STUDENTS

The new student arrivals at our universities are busy both confirming and denying stereotypes. One young chit moving into the halls of residence at Stirling University responded to a remark about the large quantity of personal gear she had brought by saying: 'Yes, I know. Daddy had to organise the family to bring all of the cars.' At the same university a very English girl was saying to her worried-looking and very English parents who were shopping with her in the supermarket: 'I told you they don't all talk like Taggart.'

A student celebrating his birthday in Glasgow's West End last week received some rather odd presents. His friend, Susie, had kindly brought him a bag containing a kaffiyeh – the Palestinian headscarf – and an umbrella. While assuming that the headscarf had been bought owing to his political sympathies, he remained perplexed about the umbrella, yet graciously accepted it on the grounds it was 'practical'. Phoning the girl in question the following day, he thanked her for the presents and asked her if she had had a good night. 'Yes,' she replied, 'but I lost my umbrella.'

A financially distressed student received a subvention from her mother after explaining she had lost her wallet in the library on Saturday night. The mother was happy to open her purse, impressed that her conscientious offspring was so immersed in her studies that she had been hunched over books late into the weekend. We wonder how generous the mother was feeling when she received a phone call from The Library bar on Sauchiehall Street, formerly the Beresford, to tell her they had found her daughter's wallet in the ladies' toilet.

☆ ☆ ☆

A Glasgow mother tells us of her birthday present from her student son. You have to picture the scene. Her son is standing in Sauchiehall Street at six in the morning after a late night in a city club, and an early breakfast in Café Insomnia. He suddenly realises that it's his mum's birthday, he hasn't bought her anything and he is about to arrive home empty-handed just as she is leaving for work. In desperation, he visits the nearest 24-hour shop in search of a solution. The happy ending sees this resourceful character stumble through the front door to present his bemused mother with a two-litre bottle of Lenor fabric softener, and a large birthday card with 'Five today' across the front, signed by himself, his three mates and the taxi driver who drove them home.

☆ ☆ ☆

Monopoly has brought out a Scottish edition, with Aberdeen as the cheapest property, which should surprise a few housebuyers there, and Balmoral – where else – in the Mayfair slot. Airline British Midland is so taken with the game they put a giant version in its lounge at Edinburgh Airport to amuse waiting passengers. A pub in Edinburgh also has one of the boards, and some visiting students were trying it out. One chap landed on Dundee and was asked for £6 in rent, but he argued: 'Don't you know the rules? You can't ask for rent in Dundee unless you have two pit bull dogs with you.' That's student humour for you.

A regular shopper in a West End supermarket much frequented by students (you can tell they are students as only students would think going to a supermarket with their mates was a day out) had picked up a box of eggs and had opened it up to check they were not damaged. As she was holding the box a student also holding a box of eggs asked her: 'Excuse me, just what is it we are supposed to be looking for?'

Colin Johnston in Aberdeen tells us of a friend who is a teacher in the city and who plays in a small jazz group in his spare time. During a break in lessons one day, he asked the pupils if they knew what jazz was. A young Aberdonian brightly answered: 'Aye, it's that film about the big shark.'

☆ ☆ ☆

A physics teacher from a Glasgow school tells us that sometimes he feels almost nostalgic for the days of the tawse. The educationalist in question was delivering a telling-off to a young female goth who had appeared in the classroom with a tad too much make-up. 'My father used to come up from the coal mine looking like that,' he told her, but was put off his stride when a voice piped up from the back row: 'What? Did he wear mascara, too?'

☆ ☆ ☆

Students across the land had all joined their university organisations for

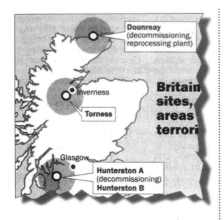

the next year, except for one slightly buxom Edinburgh girl who was telling her friend at the weekend how she had really wanted to join the skydiving club, but had been put off by the application form. 'It asked me how much I weighed, and I was afraid that if I told the usual lies something might go wrong with the parachute,' she explained.

A rather unworldly girl from Ardrossan has just started her second year at Glasgow University, but is still living down her start to tertiary education last year when she was given the course book list, and told to go to John Smith's bookshop at the university. She duly wandered into John Smith's the Bookmakers, and mystified the

punters with their roll-ups and *Racing Posts* by having a good look around and asking the cashier where the books were. But there again, we know some former students who made a similar journey, and have rarely left the premises since.

☆ ☆ ☆

A further tale of the intrusive nature of mobile phones in the country's classrooms. At one secondary school the air of industry as the pupils work hard is broken by a pupil's mobile ringing. The pupil answers it, and as his teacher approaches to remonstrate about the phone being switched on in the first place, stops teach in her tracks by saying: 'It's for you.' The teacher is rather suspicious of being the victim of some wind-up, but takes the phone and with some apprehension says 'hello'. The voice at the other end introduces herself as the pupil's mother and tells the teacher that she is just checking that her son is not playing truant.

☆ ☆ ☆

We pass on a conversation in an

Aberdeen pub where a mixed party of youthful students was discussing the expectations of women, and the question of whether an orgasm was a right and to be expected. An older chap hearing their raised voices stopped at their table on the way out and declared: 'Aye, lads, it gives them another excuse to have a moan.'

One school pupil thought religious education was a waste of time and paid little attention. His exasperated teacher told him to stand up and tell the class the Ten Commandments. The pupil hesitated so, to help him, teacher said: 'In any order you like.' So the desperate pupil finally stuttered: '8, 6, 10, 1, 4, 9, 5, 2, 7, 3.'

Graeme Hyslop, principal at Glasgow's Langside College, witnessed a little vignette of Glasgow life while popping into the Somerfield branch in Springburn of a Sunday morning. As he puts it: 'The shop boasts a very high-profile security presence which is very vocal and, by all accounts, effective. I was at the check-out when I and the bouncer noticed a local worthy helping himself to a half bottle of vodka. The

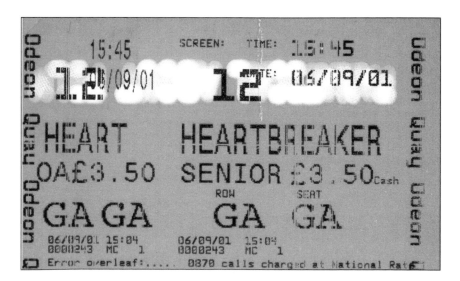

bouncer shouted "Haw yoo. Yu'r no' meant tae start knockin' the voddy tae hawf-twelve." The vodka was swiftly returned, apologies given and accepted, and Springburn returned to its normal Sunday slumbers.'

A story about *Daily Telegraph* columnist Frank Johnson complaining that he did not have an O level in Glaswegian, and therefore could not understand Speaker Michael Martin and Scots Secretary Helen Liddell, prompted Joe Winters of Robroyston to devise such an O level:

1. What do the following abbreviations stand for? a) GFT b) GTF
2. Define the following terms: a) Piece b) Party piece c) Gie's peace
3. If you went up Sauchie, doon Buchie, and alang Argyle, how many times would you be asked for money by staggering men?
4. Using a taxonomy of Glasgow marital responses, indicate a male Glaswegian's most often used reply to a spouse's enquiry as to the location of the television remote control: a) You had it last b) Up ma erse c) Ask yer maw, she's supposed tae be the oracle
5. Which of the undernoted does not belong in the sequence – fish supper/ buttered roll/ two onions/ jara mussels/ spinach/ boattle a Irn-Bru
6. Pretend that you are about to buy into the property market in Glasgow, and rate the following attributes in order of desirability: a) Ootside lavvy b) Wally close c) A nice wee single end d) Back and front door e) Drying green f) Anywhere in the West End except next door to some semi-talented prat having any connection, however tenuous, with acting, 'the dance', folk-singing, dialect revivals, puppetry or mime

More questions from the O level in Glaswegian:

When would a real Glaswegian say: 'It's a braw, bricht, moonlicht nicht the nicht'? a) Frequently, in conversation with fellow citizens b) Never, except when taking the mickey out of tourists

When is a real Glaswegian man likely to wear the kilt? a) At a wedding b) When pissed c) Over his catalogue suit trousers when pissed at a wedding

From the following list, what citizens of Glasgow might routinely address you as 'Ya bastirt'? a) Your parents and other family members b) Your friends and close colleagues at work c) Strangers

☆ ☆ ☆

There is also an Edinburgh O level. The questions include:

At Murrayfield, before the Scotland–England game, it is time to sing the national anthem. You sing: a) 'Land of Hope and Glory' b) 'God Save the Queen' c) 'Swing Low, Sweet Chariot'

Murray, Findlay, and Ogilvie are all: a) Seriously good chaps from Fettes College b) A solicitors' firm in the New Town, c) Men associated with Rangers, which is a soccer club, seemingly

A friend arrives at the door at tea-time. You say: a) Welcome in, there's plenty to go round b) You'll have had your tea c) Do you mind waiting in the parlour? Jeeves will take your fur coat d) Who are you? Get away from the door or I'll call the police

Cinzano, Bezique and Tia Maria are all: a) Jolly nice gels from finishing school b) Drinks that get you squiffy c) Seriously cool new wine bars in Stockbridge

Resentment, sadly, about the number of English students at Edinburgh University continues, particularly over those known to other students

as Yahs, who travel north from the shires due to their inability to gain entrance to Oxbridge. The latest seething disquiet is over the claim, presumably false, that the Yahs in their first year are ensconced in the costly and spacious Masson House, while the proles are billeted in the less salubrious Pollock Halls. Said one bitter student: 'The university authorities have replaced the fire alarm system at Masson House with a town crier who stands on the pavement shouting, "I say, someone's breaking into your Golf."'

SEE SPAIN, EAT THE CULTURE

Spain is full of fabulous museums, galleries, castles, palaces and sundry historical, natural and architectural wonders. I know. I have passed by many of them on my way to lunch. This may sound as if I am only interested in the food of Spain, but it is far from the truth. I also pursue with some vigour the large varieties of drink and the general ambience of fiesta which permeates the country. My favourite Spanish memories are of moments in restaurants and tapas bars, rather than at monuments.

Here are some of my favourite towns – and not presented in order of preference!

Alicante is a city so many tourists miss on their way from the airport to Benidorm. It has one of the best *carnaval* festivals in Spain. The Alicantinos take their pre-lenten bacchanal seriously. The last time I visited Alicante at *carnaval*, Peter, the proprietor of Pension Las Monges (a beautiful small hotel in a former convent), gave me a set of earplugs and a warning about the noise which would persist throughout the night. I told him I was in Alicante with the intention of adding to the noise. The *carnaval* is a wild occasion, and almost anything goes. But I was concerned by being chatted up in a queue for a toilet in a bar by a very tall redhead in a skintight dress. My anxieties were allayed when the redhead doffed the ginger wig and said: 'It's me. I'm Peter from the pension.' It would be criminal to visit Alicante without trying one of the *arroces*, or rice dishes. There is a restaurant in the marina which has

120 rice dishes on its menu, including rice with black pudding and pigs trotters. It is definitely different.

Barcelona is probably the best city in the world, but don't go there, as it's already too full of tourists.

Cadaques is a relatively unspoilt and laid-back small fishing village on the Costa Brava near the French border. It attracts many artists who think they are Salvador Dali, who lived up the road at Port Lligat. His house is now a museum, with much of the surreal master's archive, and a place of pilgrimage. When in Cadaques I make my own pilgrimage to the small restaurant where a lady called Annie introduced me first to Vina Esmeralda, a fresh and fruity wine from the Torres stable, as the perfect accompaniment to her delicious *conejo a la plancha* (grilled rabbit).

Cadiz is a big port city in the very south of Spain, next stop Africa. It hosts an extremely lively *carnaval*. Although the city is not considered a tourist venue, the people of Cadiz offer a down-to-earth, almost Glaswegian type of welcome to visitors. My abiding memory of Cadiz cuisine is of a large, old-fashioned cafe, where it seemed half the population was ensconced, consuming vast amounts of hot toast with *manteca*. *Manteca* is basically lard, and the Cadiz version contained chunks of crispy bacon. It is a heart attack on a slice of bread and sounds disgusting, but is, so to speak, to die for. Cadiz is well worth a stopover if you are on the grand tour of Andalucia.

Granada is one of the places in Spain where it is mandatory to take in the monuments. The Moorish magnificence of the Alhambra demands at least a day out of any visit. Take plenty of time to linger in the gardens and nooks and crannies of this palace/citadel. If you can afford it, and the price is not much more than a night in a bog-standard modern hotel, stay in the living history that is the Parador in the gardens of the Alhambra. The building is a 15th-century convent converted into a comfortable and atmospheric hotel. Visitors to Granada can afford to live in the Parador by saving money on food. This does not mean you will go hungry. Granada is one of the last bastions of free tapas. When you buy a drink in most of the city's bars it comes with a free morsel of food. This can range from a small dish of fried chorizo to a baked potato with alioli. My own personal best for free tapas was the night I popped into Manolo's bar in downtown Granada for an *aperitivo* on the way to have dinner. The first glass of red wine (cost approximately 30p) came with a slice of bread adorned with two small slices of bacon and a fried quail's egg. Well before the 14th and final glass of wine, Manolo and his wife Carmen in the kitchen had gone through the card of their normal free delicacies and were serving me portions of expensive *jamon*. Manolo was also pouring, gratis, glasses of Rioja from his own personal stock. I never did get to dinner.

Madrid, the capital, is without doubt the most exhausting city in Spain. The Madrilenos don't sleep, or maybe they get a nap at work. The pursuit of tapas, drink, music and *La Movida* in general is relentless. The tourist will also have to fit in visits to the Prado and other top-notch galleries. One day I'm going to catch a Velasquez or a Goya in these places. The alternative on a hot summer's day is to hang about the open swimming pool in the Casa de Campo, the park in the middle of the city. Preferably with a cold drink in the shade. The only problem is that it is full of fit young people doing acrobatic diving and stuff, which is OK if you like watching that kind of thing. Madrid, being a microcosm of all Spain, offers an astonishing range of bars and restaurants. Some of the bars, away from the main drags, offer free tapas. My favourite *bodega* offers free alternate dishes of fried fish and *patatas bravas* with each glass of wine. Four glasses of wine at about 40p each and you've had a fish supper on the house. Madrid even converted me to tripe. I had never ventured into the world of animal intestines as nourishment until I chanced upon *zarajos*. The people at the next table were eating it and it looked interesting, like a *croqueta* with strips of meat wrapped into a ball around two sticks and the whole thing deep-fried. I ordered some and it was a great discovery, crispy on the outside and pink, tender meat on the inside. Only after consuming two portions did I discover its provenance.

There are more than enough social and cultural pursuits in Madrid to keep even the most active visitor occupied, but time should be found for detours to some of the ancient towns on the outskirts of the capital. Alcala de Henares is an old university town about 30 minutes by rail from Madrid. It is the birthplace of Spain's bard, Cervantes, and is at the heart of the country's literature and culture. It is a UNESCO-designated world heritage city and you can have a pleasant day wandering around the cloisters of the various university buildings. Alcala de Henares is on a par with Granada as a free tapas location. If anything, the portions provided are bigger since the bars are used to feeding the hungry student population of 17,000. In Alcala, I had to plead with one barman to stop bringing me food with my thirst-quenching bottles of beer.

Another diverting day trip from Madrid is Segovia, about 90 kilometres from the capital. Segovia can be a more tranquil location than the more popular destination of Toledo. With its Roman aqueduct and hilly old town, it has an almost Disneyesque ambience. I must confess that it was food that made me choose Segovia over Toledo for a day trip. Juan Carlos (not the king, but a noble chap indeed) told me the *cochinillo* (slow-roasted suckling pig) was better in Segovia. The Meson Candido is the most famous purveyor of this delicacy, the patron claiming his suckling pig is tender enough to be cut with a plate. The Meson Candido is hot, crowded and touristy, and you may have to hang about for hours for a table, but it is well worth the effort.

Salamanca, another ancient seat of learning, is a two-hour train ride from Madrid. It has perhaps the loveliest main square of any city in Spain, although this can occasionally be spoiled by American students playing with frisbees or roller blading. The city is replete with foreign students. You might even meet some from the Scots College, the Roman Catholic seminary in Salamanca. It is to be hoped that the trainee Scots priests are not sampling the nightlife in Salamanca, which is relentless and relentlessly stylish. I have vague memories of being in a nightclub that was a submarine. I was drinking cava and being fed pieces of pineapple and banana with cream by a waitress. It always seems to be daylight when you get back to your *hostal*. The suckling pig is as good in Salamanca as it is in Segovia. You can get great free tapas in many bars, and there's probably a lot of culture about as well.

Most tourists think of Malaga as the airport from which you are bused down to Torremolinos, but it is also a vibrant city and a place to sample everyday Spanish life, away from the ravages of mass tourism. Malaga has great shops. They must be, if such a religiously non-shopping person as myself noticed. Tapas bars abound. Just follow your nose or start looking around a wee back street called Pasaje de Chinitas.

The highlight of any tour of Andalucia has to be Seville. The blue skies, the orange blossom, the palm-tree vistas fill the senses and lift the heart. It is steeped in history, from founding father Hercules to Generalissimo Franco. You cannot move for cathedrals, towers and other egregious architectural erections. My favourite bits are the bridges over the Quadalquivir River, from where you can imagine the Spanish ships setting out to conquer the New World. There are fabulous old *bodegas*, dusty and dark. The food tends to be simple and flavoursome, from cooling *gazpacho* to hot fried fish. Try the *tigres*. They are mussels from which the flesh has been removed, chopped up with prawn or white crab meat, stuffed back into the shell with hollandaise sauce, coated in breadcrumbs and deep-fried. A local speciality called *pringada* (at least I think it's called *pringada*; the Andalucian accent can be impenetrable at times) appealed to my Scottish predilection for offal. It is a rough paste of black pudding and other spicy sausage spread on slices of bread. I was introduced to it by a party of Seville businessmen who were working their way through a table-load of the stuff in a tapas bar. Noticing the longing looks which I was casting at their *pringada*, they invited me to join their feast. As I said, they are friendly people.

In this necessarily random selection of Spanish moments, I have so far had no room to elaborate on the fact that San Sebastian has probably the best tapas in Spain. The city is blessed with a glorious beach, usually crowded with clean-limbed, tanned, frolicsome young people. Again, OK if you can put up with that sort of thing.

I should add that Benidorm is a much-improved Costa destination. Its old town is a joy, its tapas bars packed in the winter months with Spanish *pensionistas* on a holiday paid for by their government. Please form an orderly queue here for your Spanish citizenship.

PS: I was lying about Barcelona.

LEGAL MATTERS

More tales from the courts. Sheriff Richard Davidson at Dundee Sheriff Court was dealing with a case of a chap resisting arrest. He was fined £400, and his solicitor told the sheriff that his client could pay the fine at £2.50 a fortnight. With a baleful gaze, the good sheriff told him: 'I am not collecting for a catalogue,' and upped the payments to £10.

The Scottish Courts Administration marked the Queen Mother's passing by sending out boxes of black cloth to be laid out on the benches of the country's courts as a mark of respect. Picture the scene, then, of the accused in the dock that week who went a whiter shade of pale when, before sentencing, a court official came in and began unpacking the funereal material. It was for the hyperventilating gentleman a scene too reminiscent of when judges placed a black cloth on their heads before passing the death sentence.

Just in case you forgot why Edinburgh lawyers get a bad press, we pass on the contents of an e-mail from one such lawyer when he was asked

Viagra wears off after two years

Scott Gottlieb *New York*

The anti-impotence drug sildenafil (Viagra) may stop working for many patients after two years,

for suggestions for a pal's stag night. He wrote: 'How about dwarf-throwing in Easterhouse? For £20 and a packet of Benson & Hedges, I know a chap who'll gladly strap on a helmet and let us fling him with gay abandon about a disused warehouse for half an hour. Or, alternatively, until he breaks.'

☆ ☆ ☆

Sheriff David Buchanan Smith, on retiring from the bench at Kilmarnock, would probably not thank us for reminding you that David was the 'Sash'-singing sheriff. This was widely reported as the sheriff, perhaps taking leave of his senses, singing 'The Sash' in court. In truth he was presiding over an assault case where the accused said he was provoked by the singing of 'The Sash'. Being an expert on folk

music, the good sheriff asked if it was the relatively mild version of the song, which has good folk-music traditions, or the more obscene version. The accused naturally didn't know what he was talking about, so the sheriff recited both, and a legend was born.

Our court contact tells us that sneaky Kilmarnock solicitors spread the word that Sheriff Dave was difficult to deal with, in order to scare rival Paisley solicitors from taking cases there so they could keep the fees for themselves. That can't be true, surely?

We do, however, like the story of the sheriff rebuking a solicitor whose plea in mitigation made the point that her client had kept out of trouble since 1995. The sheriff pointed out that this was hardly surprising, as he had been in jail for three of these years.

And everyone will agree with the sheriff's recent remarks on how courts should deal with ringing mobile phones – simply have a bucket of water at the ready to throw them into.

☆ ☆ ☆

Ah, the gallows humour of

lawyers. One of the chaps involved in the various legal issues surrounding the now-defunct Airdrieonians Football Club entertained his fellow fee-seekers by claiming that a female lawyer turned up at one of the meetings on behalf of a claimant, but apologised by saying: 'I'm sorry, but I'm not up to speed with agricultural law.' When asked by the other lawyers gathered there what the relevance would be, she asked them: 'It is Airdrie Onions, the name of the company, isn't it?'

An apposite mistake in the web pages of the Law Society of Scotland. In its section on divorce, common questions are listed, and under 'When can I get a divorce?' comes the answer 'If you have loved apart for more than two years.'

Alas, more apocryphal is the story of the witness being quizzed by an Edinburgh advocate depute who asked why he had gone to his friend's house that night, to be told: 'Tae get a tap.' Naturally, the confused advocate depute asked to the merriment of the court whether the accused's friend was a plumber. A colleague urgently whispered to the advocate depute, explaining local vernacular, so the advocate depute changed tack and asked: 'So you went to the house to borrow money?' Again the witness said no. At a loss he then asked in desperation: 'What kind of tap was it?' And the witness replied: 'A Rangers tap.'

A vignette from Dundee Sheriff Court where the victim, allegedly hit in the face with a glass, is called to the witness box to give evidence. After stating his name, he is then asked by the politely spoken fiscal to state his occupation. 'Criminal,' he answers with what we consider laudable frankness. He further adds to his honesty when he replies that he has no idea what happened to him as he had been 'steamin''

drunk the whole day'. Strangely enough, the fiscal failed to secure a conviction.

Our fascination with the minutiae of Dundee life as expressed in the tribulations at Dundee sheriff court knows no bounds. The latest case as reported in the *Dundee Courier* is of a deaf and mute teenager who is to face trial for contempt of court. How did he manage that? Well it seems the chap used sign language to swear at the sheriff. Or as the *Courier* put it: 'He made a gesture twice as he was being taken away by police officers and the interpreter explained what it meant.' One wonders how necessary the interpreter was.

The *Aberdeen Press and Journal* reports that one Gawain Steel was found guilty at Fort William Sheriff Court of stealing booze from his parents' holiday home. Perhaps it's just us, but is it not their own fault for calling him Gawain Steel?

We always enjoy the humour of our sheriffs, who are not as stern as they may seem. One of them was a guest speaker at a Burns supper in Lanarkshire. When he stood up he took a Get Out of Jail Free Monopoly card from his pocket and said: 'Here's something for the raffle.'

A Highland gamekeeper is cleared in the sheriff court of shooting a golden eagle, an endangered species, after his passionate plea that it was all a mistake as it had suddenly swooped down on a rabbit that he was actually aiming at. After walking free, he is stopped by the curious fiscal who asks him what had happened to the carcass. The gamekeeper explains that while he regretted shooting such a lovely bird, he nevertheless followed his father's adage of always eat what you shoot and had in fact cooked and consumed it. 'What did it taste like?' asks the curious fiscal. 'Oh,' says the gamekeeper, 'like a cross between a peregrine falcon and an osprey.'

FAMOUS FOLK

The following appeared after the official opening of the
Herald's new office in Cowcaddens, Glasgow, by the Queen.

The Queen, obviously at a loose end, popped through from Edinburgh
to the Diary call centre for a chat with Pepys the Elder. HM normally
has to ask all the questions when she meets people, which must be a
touch tedious. So, we had some questions prepared for the 30-second
encounter with the sovereign. They included: Any tips for the 3.10 at
Haydock? Is it just me or is there a terrible smell of paint in this
building? Any holidays planned or is it just hameldaeme at Holyrood
and Balmoral as usual? Have you seen much of Michael Fagan recently?
Not even a card in 20 years? Typical. I see Princess Anne's been in the
papers again. Weans! Who'd huv them?

We eventually settled for a belated thank you for that wee tin of
sweeties received in primary one in June 1953. The Queen looked
suitably baffled. A man in a suit explained the tin of sweets was a
present given to every schoolchild on the occasion of her coronation.
'That was a long time ago,' the Queen said. We could have added that
in the picture on the front of the coronation tin she was wearing a green
outfit not unlike the one she was wearing yesterday. But she had
suffered enough and graciously moved on.

It's good to get out of the city sometimes. Fred MacAulay, for example, has sneaked out of the Radio Scotland studios to take his stand-up show around Scotland, and ended up in Shetland last week. Afterwards he was approached by an eager female fan who asked him to sign her rear-end. That's the thing in those remoter parts, you just can't get a decent autograph book anywhere. Fred started scrawling his signature, and asked the fan how she enjoyed living in such a remote location without the hustle and bustle of the city. 'Och, there's regular entertainment oot here,' she replied. 'I saw Elvis last week and he signed ma erse as well.' Presumably someone who was just using her as the butt of his humour.

Writer Prue Leith was recalling in Glasgow yesterday a visit to a farm which encouraged school trips. A little nipper was holding a newly hatched chick, and with wide eyes said to the farmer: 'What will happen to him when he grows up?' Less than subtle, the farmer replied: 'In ten weeks, he will be your dinner.' Says Prue: 'I could see the teacher cringing, anxious to protect her charges from such brutality. But the boy said: "Will he be big enough then?"'

Boxing legend Ken Buchanan, rebuilding his life after the fame game went sour, told the tale of having to go back to work as a joiner when the money ran out. In his scruffy overalls not everyone recognised him, but on one job a boxing fan did indeed spot Ken and came over and asked for his autograph. He was being watched by fellow workies who did not know of his past, and one piped up in astonishment as he signed his name: 'You must be some effin' joiner.'

It was a change from the 'kent yir faither' syndrome from which all famous Scots suffer. When Billy Connolly graduated honorarily from Glasgow Yoonie he could not move for fellow graduates telling the Big Yin that their mum/auntie /granny kent him. A girl called Mairi, whose family had a connection with Connolly, made perhaps the greatest impact on the comedian. 'My mum lived round the corner from you in

Fordyce Street,' she informed Billy. Mum was duly introduced and the recognition was instant. 'You look like a Sharkey,' said the Big Yin. 'You broke my cousin's bike,' said Connolly's former neighbour. 'I did. I broke the bike,' said the Big Yin, 'but I'm 58 now. Can you no' let it go?'

Author Alasdair Gray strolled into a Glasgow West End bar for a drink and noted that a row of books were on a shelf as part of the pub's decoration. It was only when he was thumbing through one of the tomes that a member of staff shouted: 'These books are not for reading.' Dangerous thing that literature.

They try not to stare, the better class of Edinburgh folk. So when Jeffrey Archer's wife, Mary, entered the city's awfy smert Witchery restaurant with Malcolm Rifkind and his wife, other diners tried to be nonchalant. Apart from one matronly lady, who could be heard telling her dining companion: 'Well, at least she finally knows where her husband is on a Saturday night.'

Actor David Hayman, launching the scheme to sponsor seats at the Citizens' Theatre, Glasgow, was reminiscing about his first performance there as Hamlet. 'The image we had for Hamlet was that Prince Charles, the next in line to the throne, was a mental and physical wreck. During the "What is this quintessence of dust . . ." speech, I did this kind of frog leap down a very, very steep stage, and when I got to the bottom I was going so fast I went flying into the air and landed in the lap of this big woman in the front row with her two kids. She screamed at what she thought was this naked [he was actually wearing a jockstrap], sweating Hamlet who had landed in front of her. She stood up and literally threw me back up on to the stage again. I fell on my arse, stood up, and went on with the rest of the speech as if nothing had happened.' Presumably the poor woman had in mind that Shakespearian line: 'Is this a dagger I see before me?'

While Scottish Television's Stephen Jardine was out in Cannes for the film festival – yes, dirty job etc. – someone sidled up to the engineer with him and asked if the satellite dish they used could receive television pictures as well as send them. Indeed it can, said the engineer. So he was then asked if it could be arranged to download a live baseball game from the United States and relay it to a yacht in the harbour. Well, of course it could, said the engineer, who added indulgently that the satellite time for an entire baseball game would cost about the same as the national debt for a small country and the simplest thing would be to get someone to tape it and send the tape out. You don't understand, the engineer was told, Mr Nicholson likes to watch his baseball live. So a chequebook was flourished and Jack got to see his game. The phrase 'how the other half live' is hovering around here somewhere.

Middle-aged men's fantasy Nichelle Nicholls, who played the red mini-skirted Uhura in *Star Trek*, was at Glasgow's Forbidden Planet shop signing her new book. The door to the shop was temporarily closed while Nicholls chatted to staff inside, with a long queue of Trekkies developing outside. One impatient chap, clearly not a Star Trek fan, asked the security guard: 'Is it all right if normal people get into the shop?'

Irish boy-band Reel played an acoustic set at HMV in Glasgow but one band member almost didn't make it. Larging it up in Skybar the night before, the quintet attracted many admiring glances, although not always for the right reasons. 'I was at the bar acting ice cool,' said band member Philip Gargan, 'when a girl approached and said I was on fire. Thinking it was a chat-up line, I decided to move in, only for her to say, "No, you really are on fire." The hapless Irishman looked behind him only to discover that his new, waxed coat, freshly trailed over a set of candles, was ablaze.

GOT IT TAPED

A top tip which we believe we should pass on. Three young women sharing a bottle of pinot grigio in Glasgow's West End were discussing the embarrassment of going home very late after a night out when drink had been taken, and believing it was just the right time to telephone former boyfriends, even though it was three in the morning. Then one of them confided: 'I used to do it all the time, but now before I go out on a big night I cover the phone with Sellotape, and if I'm too drunk to unpick it, I can't make the call.'

Parking in Edinburgh during a rugby international weekend can be a bit of a nightmare, so we can only applaud the initiative of a Vauxhall Viva driver at an Ireland game who decided to park his clapped-out vehicle in a space reserved for a nearby company's vice-president. He was slightly perturbed, however, when a posh-looking gentleman in a Mercedes pulled into the president's space next to him, and eyed him severely. 'Excuse me,' he said, 'I don't think you're the vice-president of this place, are you?' The Viva driver was forced to admit that, no, he wasn't. 'Well, good,' said the dapper gent, walking away towards Murrayfield, 'because I'm not the president.'

The latest actor to play James Bond should be pleased with the inventiveness of the owners of a shop in Cambuslang's main street which deals in the female vanities of body piercing and sun beds. It is called Pierce Bronzin.

We have already pointed out some of the strange names that Ikea uses for its range of furniture. At the opening of its new Glasgow store a woman shopper is pondering a product called Knott and the advertising display board which says: 'Knott £7.99.' Eventually she plucks up the courage to ask an assistant: 'Well, if it's not £7.99, what price is it?'

☆ ☆ ☆

A couple are marching home in silence after being invited to the new neighbours' for dinner. Unfortunately hubby had overdone the hospitality and made a bit of a spectacle of himself. Trying to alleviate the frostiness, he turns to his silent wife and says optimistically: 'I think they're inviting us back at Christmas.' Turning sharply on her heel, she spits back: 'Whatever gave you that idea?' 'Well, I heard them saying it will be a cauld day before we're invited back,' he mutters.

☆ ☆ ☆

In one of those curious conversations that take place at a public bar, a chap in a golf polo-neck sweater tells his drinking companion: 'My doctor says I can't play golf.' His pal looks at him with concern and says: 'What? Did he discover you had some terrible ailment when he examined you?' 'No,' replied his confused companion. 'I played a round of golf with him.'

Further linguistic misunderstanding occurs when you use phrases which are common in Scotland but not so well used elsewhere. A Glaswegian couple who moved to Liverpool had a puppy which seemed a bit nervous when the new neighbours were invited in. So the lady of the house tried to put people at their ease by saying: 'It'll be OK, just give him a wee clap and he'll be happy.' And, yes indeed, after a few seconds the neighbours tentatively burst into a round of applause.

This story may well have happened in deepest Ayrshire. Two chaps go out for a spot of illegal culling of the deer population. One of them accidentally shoots his pal. He uses his mobile to phone for help. 'Ah've shot my pal. Ah think he's deid,' he blurts out to the ambulance controller. The operator, in a calm soothing voice says: 'Just take it easy. First, let's make sure he's dead.' There is a silence, then a shot is heard. The guy comes back on the line and says: 'OK, now what?'

We have chronicled linguistic misunderstandings between Scots and foreign speakers, Scots and English, even among Scots from different parts of the country. Now we hear it can even happen between couples. A chap from Darvel in Ayrshire was at a wedding with his wife when a drink or many was taken. He later found his distressed wife, Sandra, at the empty hotel reception shouting: 'Ah waant Chris. Ah waant Chris.' Fearing that she had made an inappropriate liaison due to the combination of alcohol and wedding emotions, he demanded to know who Chris was. 'Naw,' replied his unsteady partner. 'Cheese 'n' onion or salt 'n' vinegar. Ah waant chris.'

A linguistic misunderstanding, closer to home and involving not a

> Mary Doll, a spokesman for the National Park Service, said of the helicopter patrols: "They are looking at the beaches along the Outer Banks for any type of unusual activity with sharks or any other type of marine animal that might cause concern." The 27-year-old victim of the latest attack died on

foreigner but a mum. Margaret Moore tells of the time she was out for a night at the student union, an occasion which was spoiled when her bag was stolen. When Margaret arrived home, the good news was that the bag had been found. The bad news was that her mother seemed rather upset. 'Have you anything to tell me?' Mum asked with an angry visage. Margaret truthfully answered in the negative. 'Then why did your pal phone to say the gynaecologist has got your purse?' mum continued. A few inquiries with the aforementioned pal revealed the message was in fact 'the guy in the college has got your purse'.

☆ ☆ ☆

A former bookshop worker in Glasgow swears blind that celebrity gardener Charlie Dimmock was due in town to sign books, and the management had put up posters stating: 'Charlie Dimmock, the girl who can shit a slab of concrete without batting an eyelid.' It was only later that a helpful customer pointed out that the 'f' was missing from 'shift'.

☆ ☆ ☆

Our stories of linguistic misunderstandings reminded one reader of visiting a drinks party in a smart part of Sussex, where there was Pimm's served on the lawn and salmon steaks on the barbecue. After meeting the smart Sussex set, the conversation turned to accents and the difficulties that southerners sometimes have in understanding Scottish accents. One young lady piped up in polished tones that she had no problem picking up what Scots said, and although she had never been to Scotland, her mother was in fact Scottish. When asked where her mother was from, she replied in a perfect southern accent: 'Toonheid.'

The scene is the Park Bar in Glasgow where a chap from Skye is explaining the finer points of Gaelic to a local. 'There are only 17 letters in the Gaelic alphabet,' he tells him. 'There is no h, j, k, q, v, w, x, y, or z.' The Glasgow chap's face clouds over, and then he asks: 'So how do you fill out your pools coupon then?'

Overheard at Asda, Linwood. A man perusing a can of 'dolphin-friendly' tuna tells his wife: 'Get this wan – thur's nae dolphins in it.'

☆ ☆ ☆

Some confusion still exists about elements of the new dining in Glasgow's smarter restaurants. A would-be bon viveur, informed by the waitress in a Merchant City eaterie that the evening's special was 'A fillet of coley on a bed of . . .' broke in incredulously: 'You've filleted a dug?'

☆ ☆ ☆

A tale, surely not apocryphal, from an Irish toastmasters' club. There is a contest for the best short toast. A chap wins with this tribute to his spouse: 'Here's to the best years of me life, spent between the legs of me wife.' He goes home, and when his wife hears he won the contest, she is anxious to hear his winning toast. 'Here's to the best years of me life, spent in church with me wife,' he lies. The next day while out shopping, she runs into a local policeman who had also been at the meeting. He complimented her on her husband's toast. 'Well, thank you,' she replies, 'but he wasn't quite honest with all of

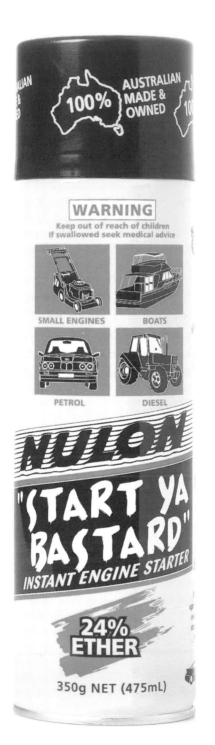

you. He's really only been there twice. The first time he fell asleep and the second time I had to drag him in by his ears.'

☆ ☆ ☆

We hear of the down-and-out who goes into the chemist's and asks to buy a bottle of methylated spirits. The chemist is dubious, saying he's not going to sell it if the chap is just going to drink it. The customer, though, argues at length that he is, in fact, a watch repairer, and the spirits are essential for cleaning watches. Finally he convinces the chemist, who puts a bottle on the counter, only to be asked: 'Have you not got a cold one in the fridge?'

☆ ☆ ☆

Practical jokes: we thought they were a thing of the past until we heard about the chap in Stirling who made a short video of his empty lavatory with his video camera. Then, when he was having a party, he waited until a nervous young woman went to said lavatory. He then told the rest of his guests to 'Watch this!' and then put on the video of the empty lavatory. On her return, the young lady saw everyone staring at the film of the empty lavatory, which she assumed was a live link, and fled the room in embarrassment.

Trying hard not to listen in, we overhear from the next table at a Glasgow wine bar: 'And after breaking off the engagement he had the cheek to want his ring back.' 'What did you tell him?' asked her anxious pal. 'Well, I just said: "In that case I want my virginity back."'

Christopher Bell, chorusmaster of the exceedingly tuneful Royal Scottish National Orchestra Chorus, is having to concede that being a Belfast man who has spent half his life in Belfast and half in Scotland has left him with an accent that not everyone can decipher. It would explain why, after arriving early for a Scottish Opera costume sale and going for a cup of coffee, he found himself in need of using the loo. Approaching the receptionist, he asked: 'Where can I pee?' only to be told: 'There's no need, it's free admission.'

You can take the boy out of the council house but you can't take the council house . . . An Ayrshire lady tells of a friend who was preparing food for a barbecue. Her husband offered to undertake the marinating or, as he actually put it, he'd 'away and steep the chicken' for her.

The Diary continues to warm to the goths and moshers who congregate outside the Gallery of Modern Art in Glasgow. We are told that one such teenage boy, dressed in black with green hair and a stud in his nose, casually explained after an inquiry about his attire: 'I don't really like to wear this gear, but it keeps my parents from dragging me everywhere with them.'

A trade union official overheard discussing the oratorical skills of a colleague: 'Can he think on his feet? If he'd been captain of the Titanic, he would have told the passengers the ship had only stopped to take on ice.'

The hot weather helped a Glasgow East Ender recall a previous bout of sunshine when a handyman was sent to mow the extensive grass around a local church. Because of the heat, he invested in a can of lager as he worked, and then another one, and then another one, until he was found by the minister asleep inside the church, the grass largely untouched. The fed-up clergyman shook him awake and remonstrated with him about the state he was in. Clutching at straws, the chap attempted to placate the minister with: 'Jesus liked a drink.' 'Aye,' said the minister. 'But not in my vestry, he didn't.'

We are told it is true that a teacher in Ayrshire was trying to cope with a severely sprained ankle and that her concerned husband, wanting to help her as much as possible, sawed the legs off her ironing board so she could iron with it on her lap. Caring, Ayrshire style.

We would never make light of a missing pet, an event that can cause real grief. But we were slightly intrigued to note a plea in the 'Lost and Found' which read: 'Lost in Dalmarnock area, boxer dog with tail . . .' We presume it is unusual for a boxer to have a tail, not for a dog in Dalmarnock to have one.

A science teacher swears blind to us that when he asked his class: 'What's inertia?' some bright spark answered, 'Troon and Prestwick.'

Campaigners trying to save Govanhill Baths resorted to a bit of poster hijacking by changing the wording on Tory billboards on the south side of Glasgow. It was the series which read 'You've paid the taxes', and at the bottom the campaigners painted over the Tory wording and added, 'So where are the baths?' They were working on a poster of an Asian father with his two children with the message, 'So where are the schools?', when a chap drove up in a car and asked what they were doing. 'You're not painting over the faces, are you?' he asked. When they assured him they were just tampering with the wording he said that was a relief, as it was himself who was in the poster and he had brought his children along to see it.

A doorstep tale from Dundee. One early Saturday, a denizen of Clootie City arose and went to answer the doorbell, clad in vest, and eyes still pink from the vodka the night before. In front of him were two crew-cuts, two youthful faces, and two sober dark suits: clearly a pair of young gentlemen of the Mormon persuasion. 'Good morning,' one said. But before he could go on, he was interrupted: 'Whoa,' said the householder. 'Have you come tae me wi' a message fae God?' The youngster's face lit up: 'Well, yeah, we have.' 'Well, beat it,' replied the Dundonian. 'Eh dinnae deal wi' middlemen.'

It is becoming habit-forming peeking into the logbook at Scottish Television, so we must stop it. But just before we do, we give you one more insight into the thought-processes of some viewers. The log tells us: 'The viewer has taught her budgie to say Angus Simpson. She thinks this is potentially the biggest TV moment of the decade, and for a nominal fee will allow us to film the bird. She is also keen to discuss the obvious potential spin off, i.e. the budgie getting its own show.' Alas, the entry is stamped: 'No response required.' A great idea going a-begging, we reckon.

☆ ☆ ☆

Some confusion as a *Scotland Today* cameraman, Clive Woods, is

dispatched to film an interview with Martin Raymond of the Health Education Board for Scotland, or HEBS as it is known. Mr Raymond is waiting at his Edinburgh HQ for the arrival of the cameraman. When contacted on his mobile phone, Mr Woods says that he, too, is waiting for the arrival of the HEBS man. 'Where are you?' Mr Woods is asked. 'Easter Road, of course,' he replies. This is reminiscent of the time Tommy McLean, then manager of Heart of Midlothian FC, is in Edinburgh Airport with his assistant coach, Tom Forsyth, waiting for a flight. A voice over the Tannoy asks for 'a Hertz representative' to come to the phone. Tommy McLean says: 'I suppose we'd better go and find out what they want.'

A chap in an Edinburgh bar having an après-work pint asked his colleagues: 'Can I have a fag?' His mate with the ciggies quite reasonably pointed out to the chap that he had in fact just recently given up smoking. 'Well, I'm in the process of quitting. I'm in the middle of phase one right now.' When his confused pal asked what phase one was, he replied: 'I've stopped buying.'

MEDICAL MATTERS

Overheard in the outpatient clinic of the cardiac treatment ward of a Glasgow hospital was a wee wumman who was telling the person next to her, as you do, that when questioned on her lifestyle, she admitted smoking a packet of fags a day and having a wee drink or two every night to help her sleep. As she went on to explain: 'They wur mad aboot ma smokin'. They said, "Yu'll have tae stoap that smokin'." When Ah said tae them: "Dae ye no care aboot ma drinkin'?" they said: "Naw, hen. That's Livers."'

Aspiring Scottish psychiatrists were attending their first class on emotional extremes at Glasgow University. 'Just to establish some parameters,' said the professor to the student from Giffnock, 'what is the opposite of joy?' 'Sadness,' said the student. 'And the opposite of depression?' he asked of the young lady from Kelvinside. 'Elation,' she said. 'And you, sir,' he said to the young man from Kilwinning, 'how about the opposite of woe?' Naturally he replied: 'Giddy up.'

A reader who met some nurses from Stobhill Hospital heard them using the strange medical term 'jesters' shoes'. He inquired as to the meaning, and they explained that the phenomenon occurs when nervous chaps are lying

on the operating table awaiting a vasectomy, and the surgeon approaches to give a local anaesthetic injected into somewhere very private. Apparently many a patient's toes instinctively curl back against the shins as the needle goes in – hence the term 'jesters' shoes'.

A Coatbridge chap who was in Monklands Hospital for a few days for a minor operation had to fill in the daily card stating what he wanted to eat for lunch and dinner the next day. As he was hopefully being discharged in the next 24 hours, he left the card blank, which was queried by the bustling auxiliary. He started to explain: 'I don't think I'll be here tomorrow,' but she interrupted, patted him consolingly, and told him: 'That's no way to talk.'

MP Ming Campbell's campaign for real nappies strikes a chord with Fiona McMillan, who believes there is a genuine need to educate young people about the real variety rather than the disposable types. She tells us: 'When he was about five months old, I had to take my son, Duncan, who was suffering from severe constipation, for an X-ray. When it came to looking at the result the young registrar exclaimed, "No wonder he's in pain, look what he's swallowed." I then had to point out that he still had his terry nappy on, and she was looking at an X-ray of a nappy pin.'

How to win over your audience. The compères at a charity fashion show put on by students in Dundee to raise money for Ninewells Hospital's special baby care unit told some less than complimentary jokes about the city by the Tay. One of them said he was dating a girl from Dundee, and added: 'I knew she was single – she had a child.' The silence was deafening.

☆ ☆ ☆

MEDICAL MATTERS

A reader very fond of his old aunty tells us of taking her to the Stobhill Hospital fracture clinic for a follow-up appointment. He had to suppress a smile when the doctor, carefully examining the healing bone, asked her: 'When did you break your wrist?' In all earnestness she replied: 'When I fell, Doctor.'

Our story of the junior doctor who believed that a baby had swallowed a large pin when the X-ray showed up its nappy fastener reminded a retired radiographer of a colleague who was asked by a doctor to repeat an X-ray of a lady patient, 'but this time without the bedspring showing'. It was pointed out to the young medic, to his discomfiture, that the image prominent on the film was not a bedspring, but a contraceptive coil.

The scene is an ER department in Aberdeen where a doctor has been called to administer an anaesthetic to a hungover 16-year-old male (easily diagnosed as NED-positive) who was nursing a swollen hand. The patient insisted he had damaged it by punching a phone box but, given the marks on his knuckles and the livid inflammation, it was obvious that this particular phone box came fitted with a full set of human teeth. Accepting that she wasn't going to get any further details regarding the injury, she proceeded with the standard formal questions, beginning with asking whether he had been to theatre before. 'Aye,' he replied. 'I saw yon *Peter Pan* at His Majesty's. But fit's that got tae dae wi' onythin'?'

A reader prescribed Propranolol by his doctor was struck by the long list of possible side-effects on the leaflet which accompanied the tablets. These potential complications include breathlessness or wheezing, dizziness or fainting, dry eyes, skin troubles such as rashes or itching, unexplained allergic reactions, heart problems (such as heart failure and heart block), a very slow heart rate, low blood pressure, poor circulation, blood disorders (often characterised by pallor, fever, unusual bleeding or unexplained bruising), pain in the calf muscles, nightmares, visual disturbances, mood changes, cold or numb fingers or toes, feeling or being sick, diarrhoea, pins-and-needles, tiredness and insomnia, severe mental problems, and hair loss. The medicine had been prescribed to alleviate the patient's feelings of anxiety.

Do we believe the Glasgow doctor who claims he told a patient recovering from heart surgery that he would be able to resume a normal sex life as soon as he could climb two flights of stairs without being out of breath, and that his patient frowned before replying: 'What if I look for a wummin who lives on the ground floor?'

First Aid is a serious business, and could easily save someone's life, so we were not amused by a chap in Glasgow who was sent on a course by his firm. The class was being taught resuscitation on a Resusci-Annie, a rubber model which only goes down to the torso to make it easier to transport. When our bold lad was asked to have a shot, he walked over, put his ear to her mouth to listen for breathing, then announced to the class: 'She says she can't feel her legs!'

A dental practice in Ayr run by four chaps is telephoned by a directory and asked for the names of the partners. Just as it is printed on the practice's letterhead, the directory is told: 'J.N. Stevenson, K. Ross, M.E. Geller and F.E. Tait.' So the following week *Who's Who in Dentistry* writes to say that Jane Stevenson, Kay Ross, Emmie Geller and Effie Tait will be included in the next edition. Norrie Stevenson says they draw the line at putting on dresses to go to work, particularly as the surgery is in Queens Court.

Kiain Balloch, who works for the health service in Stirling, passes on a doctor's letter from the normally dry publication *Clinical Guidelines In Practice*. The doctor writes: 'I saw a woman who'd

been in hospital for a routine operation. I hadn't had a letter back from the surgeon so I asked, "What did the doctor tell you?" "He said I was going home to die." She looked quite well on it, but I presumed they'd found something awful when they opened her up, so we had a long chat about making wills and pain relief. When I got back to the surgery, I called the doctor for more details. He was very surprised – and very Australian: "I told her she was going home today."'

☆ ☆ ☆

An Aberdeen woman had just given birth, and the nurse, cradling the baby in her arms, asked what she intended to call it. 'Nathan,' replied the panting mother, prompting the nurse to squawk: 'Bit you've got tae call it something . . .'

☆ ☆ ☆

We hear of a story surrounding the opening of a new pharmacy in Clydebank. There was a great amount of anticipation in the area as to when it would open and who the chemist would be. At the nearby community centre, a group of local mums were gathered, when in rushed an excited local with information. In the Clydebank vernacular, the woman exclaimed: 'The new chemist is sellin' Es.' This caused a measure of uproar among the throng but, before a posse of vigilantes could be mustered to challenge the chemist for encouraging drug-taking in the area, it was clarified that the young lady was actually from another part of the Commonwealth and was, in fact, Ceylonese.

It's not much fun being a butcher these days, but Kenny the butcher in Partick attempts to entertain the Saturday morning queue by announcing: 'Did you hear about the chap who answered a knock at the door and found a six-foot spider standing there?' He then went on to explain to the listening housewives queuing for their shoulder steak and links that the giant spider abruptly nutted the

poor chap then leapt on him, breaking four of his ribs. When he came round in hospital, completely bemused, he asked the doctor what had happened. Shaking his head, the doc told him: 'There's a nasty bug going around.' Naturally all were tempted to tell Kenny to stick to his day job.

Greater access to their hospital files by patients will lead alas to doctors tidying up their acronyms in their notes. In one Edinburgh hospital the irritating last patient of the week is known as a Loofa – or last one on a Friday afternoon. Patients who don't respond to any treatment sometimes have 'teeth' written in their notes. It stands for tried everything else, try homeopathy. There is also the intriguing NFF – or Normal for Fife.

TRAVEL MATTERS

Someone not clear on the concept just after the Euro is introduced. A chap from Springburn is just back from a New Year holiday in Dublin. He turns to his pals back in Glasgow and tells them: 'See the Irish and their punts? They were spending them as if they were going out of fashion.'

We add to our collection of apocryphal stories with this one, which is supposed to have happened to a lucky Scot flying from New York to London. A man boards a plane and takes his seat. As he settles in, he glances up and sees a beautiful blonde boarding the plane. He can hardly believe his luck as she makes her way towards his seat. A wave of nervous anticipation washes over him as, lo and behold, she takes the seat right beside him. Eager to strike up a conversation, he blurts out: 'Business trip or vacation?' 'Nymphomaniac convention in London,' she states. His eyes dart nervously from the back of the seat in front of him to the air conditioning unit above him, as he struggles to control his excitement. Eventually, he asks what her role is at the convention, to which she replies that she is a lecturer, before adding: 'I use my experiences to debunk some of the popular myths about sexuality.' 'Really,' he says, swallowing hard. 'What myths are those?' 'Well,' she explains, 'one popular myth is that African-American men are the most endowed when, in fact, it is the native American Indian who's most likely to possess that trait. Another popular myth is that Frenchmen are the best lovers, when actually it is men of Scots descent.' Suddenly, the woman gets a bit embarrassed and blushes. 'I'm sorry,' she says. 'I shouldn't be discussing this with you. I don't even know your name.' 'Tonto,' the man replies. 'Tonto Macpherson,' he adds, extending his hand.

A Texan visiting Scotland is bragging about the size of the state he comes from, and tells his bored audience: 'In Texas you can get on a train, ride all day long, and still be in Texas by nightfall.' Which allowed a weary Scots listener to tell him: 'Aye, we've got these rotten trains on the Glasgow to Edinburgh run as well.'

Ian Watt of Carnoustie tells us of being in a bar in Edinburgh's Rose Street with a friend on holiday from England who was getting confused about the difference between Scottish pound notes and fivers. Eventually the chap told the patient barman waiting for his money: 'You'll have to excuse me, I'm English.' And with a deadpan delivery, the barman replied: 'That's OK sir, we get all sorts in here.'

Further linguistic misunderstandings as we hear of the Perth prison officers discussing a trip to Paris that one of them is planning. He went on to explain that he and his wife love Paris and visit frequently. 'Oh,' says his colleague in an admittedly strong Fife accent. 'You'll be fluent then?' 'Nah', says his colleague, 'driving and then the ferry. The wife doesn't like aeroplanes.'

Raymond McIntosh of Bankfoot, Perthshire, was recalling happier days of flying across the Atlantic. While going from Glasgow to LA, he and his wife changed planes at Chicago, and decided to check that the connection would be announced over the loudspeaker, as they once almost missed a plane because nothing was announced. So his wife approached the charming girl at the American Airlines desk and, in her poshest tones, asked: 'Excuse me. Could you tell me if our flight will be called?' After a slight pause, the girl replied: 'Gee, no ma'am. All our flights are air-conditioned.'

That reminded one reader of a story – which he swears is true – of an American family touring the Highlands. They stopped at a small pub to sample some of the 'local fayre', which included a chicken tikka for the father. Halfway through the meal, the attentive waiter approached and asked the mother: 'Can I get you anything else, madam?' 'No, everything's just fine, thanks.' 'Curry OK, sir?' he asked the father, which prompted the bewildered reply: 'No thanks. I can't sing a note, anyway.'

A Scots businessman who returned post 9/11 from Australia says he witnessed a fellow business chap's most embarrassing moment which is probably still making him cringe. They were part of a group being shown around a large new extension to the Adelaide Convention Centre when the bloke next to him thoughtlessly blurted out: 'It's so huge, you could get a jumbo jet in here.'

The humour of pilots can frequently be a bit dubious. Reader Sam Mackie was on a plane about to land at Glasgow when he heard the captain say over the microphone to the crew: 'Spanish doors, Spanish doors everyone.' After a minute he then announced to the passengers: 'Doors to Manuel, doors to manual.' Oh, how they laughed – apart from the Spanish, of course.

The dodgy humour of airline crews continues, with Sandy Smith recalling a flight from Norway to London when the steward reached the point about oxygen masks dropping from above and the need to put your own mask on before helping your child. The attendant then added: 'If travelling with more than one child, you should first secure your own mask and at that time decide which one you love most.'

Diary reader Ewan Orr avows that while visiting America he became engrossed in the country music channel TNN (The Nashville Network) when a female singer came on and was chatting about a recent European tour she had embarked on. Explaining that although it had all gone well, there was one apprehensive moment before a concert when she thought the audience were all being sick. This was because she had asked a stagehand before going on what the audience was like and he had replied: 'It's heavin' out there darlin'.' The venue was indeed Glasgow.

A plane was about to land at Glasgow Airport with the captain giving the usual chat over the intercom about local weather conditions and where you can hire a car, when he suddenly cried: 'Oh, my God!' After an uncomfortable silence he came back on to say: 'Sorry, ladies and gentlemen, but I was just handed a cup of tea by the steward which I dropped. You should see the front of my trousers.' And the Glasgow passenger listening to this murmured to his pal: 'That's nothing. You should see the back of mine.'

Willie Maley from Ayr was flying back to London from Barcelona when he noticed a mature woman, whom he later discovered came from Glasgow, struggling to put a traditional-style broom into the overhead locker. It's the sort of thing they make so well in Barcelona and you can never seem to get here. Anyway, the stewardess, trying to get everyone seated, bustled up and, in that haughty cabin staff way, asked: 'What on earth is this for?' Naturally the Glasgow woman replied: 'What do you think it's for?' And then, in a moment of genius, added: 'It's in case I have to leave the plane in flight.'

CHRISTMAS MATTERS

Are you the type of person who blames others when you are late? Perhaps the sundial received by Sheila Madsen as a Christmas present is for you. The instructions explain: 'When properly installed, your sundial will show accurate solar time. If your dial is running fast or slow it is not the fault of the dial, it is caused by the motion of the earth around the sun.'

A Glasgow reader who decided on a quiet Christmas on the beautiful island of Colonsay tells us she was quite startled on the ferry over when she heard a local woman tell her companion: 'Alistair is a fantastic man. He must have given crabs to every woman in the village.' Sadly, it's the way the Glasgow mind works.

Nerves get stretched in shops at Christmas. That is probably why a young woman is asking her friend why she lost her job in the department store. 'Honest to God, this woman must have tried on over a dozen dresses before she said she thought she would look nicer in something more flowing. So I suggested the Clyde.'

Wishaw General Monday Lunch Menu Week 1

To make your selection, place a 🗑 in the appropriate box.

Since most people will be groaning under the weight of their hangovers, we thought we'd add to the noise with the news that there was a transvestite who was desperate to get into the Glasgow Hogmanay street party. Apparently, he really wanted to eat, drink and be Mary.

☆ ☆ ☆

For those going to a New Year party, here is a rough guide to cut out and keep which will let you know when it is time to go home: You notice your tie sticking out of your fly. You strike a match and light your nose. You start kissing the portraits on the wall. You hear a duck quacking and it's you. You announce you are going home – but the party is at your place. You ask for another ice cube and put it in your pocket. You yawn at the biggest bore in the room – then realise you're in front of the hall mirror. You tell your best joke to the rubber plant. You realise you're the only one under the coffee table.

☆ ☆ ☆

The traditional Christmas shopping scene. A confused chap is standing in the queue at the Virgin record store in Glasgow's Buchanan Street. He has been sent into town with a shopping list. He is asking for a copy of *Straight and Strong* by Baby Bliss for his daughter. The assistant has never heard of it. He searches the computer database and still nothing. The chap hands over his list, and sure enough it is written down. At that a female assistant walks past, glances at the list and announces: 'Babyliss's Straight and Strong? It's a hair iron. You'll get it in Boots.' And off shuffles the embarrassed chap, muttering about never doing the Christmas present-buying again.

A card assistant noticed a chap who had been lingering at the anniversary cards for some time, so she finally asked if there was a problem. 'Yes, there is,' he replied mournfully. 'I can't find one my wife will believe.'

We are told of the frantic Christmas shopper picking through the frozen turkeys in the supermarket but unable to find one large enough for the extended family descending on her home this year. So she asks the youthful shop assistant strolling past: 'Do these turkeys get any bigger?' His brow furrowing, he tells her: 'No. They're deid.'

☆ ☆ ☆

Our stories about record shop misunderstandings reminded Fraser Jenkins of the time his granny ventured into HMV in Glasgow to buy him a CD. She had written down that he wanted a particular album by Iron Maiden, and, failing to spot it, she asked an assistant where she would find it. The assistant did his best, by telling her it would be in the heavy metal stand near the back of the shop. A flustered gran returned to the desk after another fruitless search in order to tell the assistant: 'You'll need to help me son. I can't see any metal stands – only wooden ones.'

☆ ☆ ☆

After observing the mêlée at Braehead shopping centre, we pass on the following rules for Christmas parking:

When another vehicle is waiting for you to pull out of a parking space when it is busy, take your time. Adjust the mirrors, your seat, and the radio. Feel free to go through your shopping bags and look at what you just bought.

If a shopping trolley is near your car, simply push it in the opposite direction towards some other cars, and keep on walking.

If you are filling your car with shopping, but are going back in for more, don't tell the driver who is sitting patiently waiting to take your space.

When walking back to your car, if you notice other shoppers walking past your car to get to theirs, press the button on your key which makes the alarm go 'bloop bloop'. With luck it will scare the wits out of them.

If you don't see a speed limit sign in the car park, there isn't any.

When leaving a shopping centre at a busy road, go through the narrow 'enter only' driveway, stick the front of the car into traffic, and wait.

Always leave your shopping trolley behind or between parked vehicles.

Empty your ashtray on the ground, and while you're at it, dump out all the rubbish, too, including that McDonald's bag the kids have left on the back seat.

If you are forced to change a disposable nappy, remember to leave the old one below the car next to you.

☆ ☆ ☆

Our readers add more:

Parking bays with a wheelchair symbol are often conveniently sited adjacent to main entrances. People with mobility problems don't mind able-bodied persons taking their place.

Whenever possible, park as close as you can to the driver's door of the car in the next bay. People enjoy clambering into their car through the passenger door and will be grateful for the exercise.

If you can't find a space quickly, you can park anywhere you like as long as you switch your hazard lights on. People will realise you are far too important to follow normal rules and will be happy to squeeze round you.